TURNING
TEXAS BLUE

TURNING

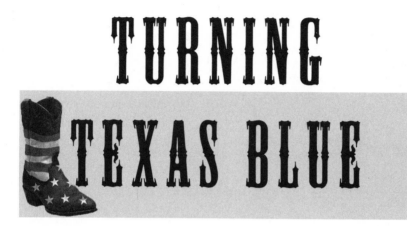

TEXAS BLUE

What It Will Take to Break the GOP
Grip on America's Reddest State

MARY BETH ROGERS

St. Martin's Press
New York

www.stmartins.com

Cataloging-in-Publication Data is available from the Library of Congress.

ISBN 978-1-250-07908-4 (hardcover)
ISBN 978-1-4668-9171-5 (e-book)

Design by Letra Libre, Inc.

Our books may be purchased in bulk for promotional, educational, or business use. Please contact your local bookseller or the Macmillan Corporate and Premium Sales Department at (800) 221-7945, extension 5442, or by e-mail at MacmillanSpecialMarkets@macmillan.com.

First Edition: January 2016

10 9 8 7 6 5 4 3 2 1

For

Billy and Eleanor

My children of vision and courage

Contents

Introduction	Why It Matters	1
One	Reality of Defeat—One More Time	13
	So Close and Still So Far	
	The Davis Dilemma	
Two	Lessons of 2014	29
	Battleground or Battle-Scam?	
	The Amway Plan	
	Did It Matter?	
Three	Rise of the Outsiders	43
	The Texas Way	
	The New Deal and Birth of the Modern Republican Party	
	Liberals on the Horizon	
	Sudden Opening	
Four	Blame It on Perot—and on Liberals, Too	59
	Voting Rights Act for All	
	Liberals Hit the Jackpot	
Five	Permanent Breakthrough	73
	Aces in the Hole	
	Catalyst for Change	
	The Gang of Four	

Six   The Illusion of Victory   87
          A New Texas Experiment
          Perils of Frustration and Fatigue
          Slow Learners in a Fast-Moving Game
          Dream Team Turns Nightmare

Seven   Clowns, Crackpots, and
          Christian Crusaders   107
          The Education of Tom Luce
          The Political Genius of Rick Perry—Really!
          The Confrontation
          The Punisher
          Leaks in the Big Red Bubble

Eight   Hispanics—Hype and Hope   133
          Is Karl Rove Right?
          The Hispanic Face of Republicanism
          We Just Can't Get Rid of the Bushes
          The Mother of Hope: Rosie Castro and
              Her Boys

Nine   A New Texas Way   159
          The Pope Effect
          The Dreamers
          Plague of Internal Conflicts
          The New Suburbia
          How Dallas Became a Democratic Stronghold
          Money—It's Always the Money!

Ten   Memo to the Future   185
          Dear Texas Democrats . . .

          Afterword   211

          Acknowledgments   217
          Notes   221
          Bibliography   233
          Index   237

TURNING
TEXAS BLUE

INTRODUCTION

Why It Matters

THIS IS A STORY ABOUT HOW CHANGE CAN occur in Texas; how Texas might turn blue—the telltale word in our political parlance that has reduced complicated politics to primary colors. There are times when I'd like to strangle the graphic designer who created red and blue television maps to show which party was winning each state on election night. By 2000, it was clear that we Democrats had been designated the cool blue team and the Republicans got to be the red-hots. And now, we're stuck with that. But maybe it's better than being donkeys or elephants. It all depends on your point of view.

Democrats are not very cool in Texas these days—and haven't been for a long time.

In 1990 I ran the last campaign to put a Democrat in the Texas governor's office—the late, great Ann Richards. Four years later, I ran her reelection campaign, which she lost, giving George W. Bush a high-profile perch from which to begin his troublesome tenure in American politics. I've seen both sides of Texas politics—euphoric victory and bitter loss. In the twenty years since that big loss, I've watched ordinary, business-oriented, conservative Republicans morph into crackpots and blustery buffoons. Many of us here didn't figure out the extent of their damage until we were so deep in a hole that we didn't know how to get out. That's because the Republican takeover of Texas has actually been a long, slow slog that crept up on us and has now left behind a path of political destruction and debris that desperately needs a good Democratic cleanup crew.

After decades of watching from a distance, I'm just plain tired of waiting for that crew to magically arrive and bring back sanity, common sense, and decency to politics and policy in my state. So I decided I better start thinking about how to find a shovel to dig us out of this hole, instead of fuming and fussing as most of my Democratic friends do. Besides, I'm tired of feeling guilty that I wasn't savvy enough back in 1994 to prevent Bush and his Republican enablers from embarking on their calamitous journey through Texas and the world.

Texas, of course, is the reddest of the red-hot states, covered by a big bubble that protects the most reactionary, radical, and rabid set of officeholders that much of the country has ever seen. Hot red wind escapes the bubble every once in a while and blows out of Texas onto the rest of you. If you even casually watched the bizarre buildup to the 2016 Republican presidential primaries, you might have noticed the Texas blowhards who wanted your votes—Rick Perry, Ted Cruz, and the Texas-bred guys who grew up here with famous fathers: Jeb Bush and Rand Paul.

All of this has been brought to you by the total Republican takeover of Texas state government—from top to bottom. Within four short years after George W. Bush's defeat of Ann Richards, Republicans had won every statewide elected office and almost obliterated the Texas Democratic Party, which is hanging by a thread today.

The rest of the country had better hope that cool blue winds prevail in Texas sooner rather than later because we've got a new crop of politicians here just waiting to bring you their special brand of crazy—the kind that encourages men to bring their Glocks to shopping malls, teachers to use Bibles as schoolbooks, and oil companies to put drilling rigs in your front yard. Luckily, these guys aren't hard to spot. They identify themselves as former "pre-born fetuses" and promise to prevent your children from learning about evolution, or climate change, or anything resembling an accurate version of American history.

In the past twenty years, their takeover of Texas has set in motion practices, policies, and politics that have spread like an unchecked virus all over the country. See something crazy in Wisconsin or Indiana? It probably started in Texas. Want it to stop in your state? It's probably going to have to stop in Texas first.

While my story is primarily about the Lone Star State, it also has national implications. There is something in the atmosphere here that convinces politicians that they should be president of the United States. In the past 50 years, three of them made it: Lyndon B. Johnson, George Herbert Walker Bush, and George W. Bush. But Texas's impact on the nation doesn't end with presidents.

Just look at the national Tea Party movement and you will see the mark of a Texan—Dick Armey, the former majority leader in the U.S. House of Representatives. Armey was probably the most significant original booster of the Tea Party movement in the nation. His FreedomWorks organization funded, trained, advised, and supported Tea Party leaders and the populist rallies that brought them fame. The movement was nourished by Texas money and inflamed and encouraged by the rhetoric of its most extreme members.

Keep looking and you will find Texan Tom DeLay, the disgraced former House Republican whip known as "The Hammer." DeLay banged out the wildly successful redistricting redo after the 2000 census. His gerrymandering scheme created so many safe Republican congressional districts in Texas and other states that there is no incentive for conservatives to move to the center in order to win the hearts, minds, or support of independent voters. Fed up with congressional gridlock? Blame Texan Tom DeLay.

Almost worse, it was in Texas that the origins of today's megadonor control of American politics was birthed and built. The practice, perfection, and power of "special purpose" individual expenditure campaign committees were fine-tuned in the Lone Star State. Small groups of megadonors, pushing their personal or political agendas, went largely unnoticed until 2004 when Karl Rove's Texas group spent more than $10 million on the "Swift Boat" campaign against Democratic presidential candidate John Kerry.[1] The ads managed to take Kerry's strength as a Vietnam War hero and turn it into a liability by twisting the truth of his experiences. The tactic proved so effective that it triggered the desire of other conservative billionaires across the country to use their money and power in similar efforts. Rich people have always used their wealth to influence politics. But the individual expenditure committees allowed them to advance their self-interest in a new, more effective way, totally independent of their favorite candidates. Of course, the U.S. Supreme Court's 2010 decision in the *Citizens United* case quickly gave them absolute legal permission to do so. Since then, buying political power has taken on a unique Texas twist—largely because of Rove's post–Oval Office career as fundraising guru to America's wealthy conservative donors.

Look deeper into Texas political history and you will find the real reason the tort reform movement spread from Texas throughout the nation. Texas was one of the first states to restrict the ability of ordinary citizens to seek redress for personal injury or negligent medical mistakes. The movement started in Texas in the early 1980s with a dual purpose: one, to shield corporations, doctors, and medical institutions from having to pay for their mistakes or malfeasance; and, two, to drive plaintiff lawyers—longtime major funders of Democratic campaigns—out of business. After George W. Bush became governor, the effort went forward with full steam. When anti-tax advocate Grover Norquist saw how Texas had dried up a source of income for the state's trial lawyers and almost killed off Democratic Party fund-raising in Texas, he advised other states to follow suit. He claimed that the most essential element in "defunding" the Democratic Party at the state and national levels was the enactment of tort reform.[2] It worked particularly well in Texas, and it is one reason why Democrats here have been unable to raise enough money to bring their party back to viability.

Of course, there is George W. Bush himself, who left a wide swath of tragedy in his wake—the wars and turmoil in the Middle East that have claimed hundreds of thousands of lives, the bungled response to Hurricane Katrina, and the economic recession that upended middle-class lives and increased the nation's income gap. Meanwhile, his No Child Left Behind education legislation, in addition to degrading teachers and distressing parents, has led to the creation of a multi-billion-dollar testing industry, a "no public dollar left unspent" debacle that has done little to help the nation's children perform at levels comparable to those of most of the modern industrial world.

Like it or not, Texas matters.

But will it ever change?

Of course it will. Politics in Texas is like its weather—a tornado disaster one day and sunny skies the next. It's just been an unusually long storm season.

When the wind shifts, as it inevitably will, Texas's political fortunes will have a profound effect on how both Democrats and Republicans "run the numbers" in the Electoral College to actually win the presidency. Republicans obviously want to keep Texas a deep shade of red to hold on to its 38 electoral votes. If Democrats were to pry Texas loose and make it a genuine swing state like Florida, the whole dynamics of presidential campaign politics would change. A strategy to win the presidency requires securing the popular vote in enough states to win their allocated votes in the Electoral College. Like it or not, some states matter more than others. That's because the number of votes they have in the Electoral College is based on their population.

Take California, for example. When that state's prized 55 electoral votes became a sure thing for Democrats after 1992, Republicans had to scramble to win votes in states like Pennsylvania or Michigan that had strong Democratic voting histories, or they had to put together combinations of smaller state victories sufficient to make up the difference. That's not easy, as the last two presidential elections have demonstrated. If Texas were to flip, Republicans would have an even more difficult time implementing an effective Electoral College strategy. On the other hand, Democrats are finding that they may actually need to win Texas to assure their own prospects. Their much-heralded 2012 presidential victories in states like Colorado, Virginia, Iowa, and Ohio were so close as to provide no guarantee for future victories. And the 2014 losses for Senate Democrats in other states prove how precarious their hold could be in the next presidential election. At some point in the not-too-distant future, national Democrats are going to have to think differently about Texas.

All of the hotshot experts know this. They've spent years looking at the shifting minority demographics and actively debating when the blue wave might overtake Texas. Some think change could occur in time for the 2016 presidential election—but then, this state's political battlefield is littered with the bodies of consultants and candidates who thought they knew how to turn the tables in Texas. Still, that did not deter some of those experts from wading into Texas one more time.

In 2013, a group of victorious 2012 Obama operatives thought they could work their campaign magic to bring Texas into play for 2016. Jeremy Bird and his 270 Strategies Consulting Group came to Texas to create a new grassroots organization called Battleground Texas. The purpose was clearly revealed in the group's name: 270 is the magic number of votes to win a majority in the Electoral College, and thus the presidency. Bird had been Obama's national field director in 2012. After the election, Bird and Mitch Stewart, along with other high-level Obama operatives, set up a consulting firm and landed clients like Planned Parenthood, the Service Employees International Union (SEIU), and the Ready for Hillary super PAC. All the while Bird kept his eyes on Texas—a new challenge and a new political client.

He had looked at Texas's exploding Hispanic population and realized that if he could make the voting electorate look like the population, he could turn Texas blue. Democrats had already begun making strides in key urban areas like Dallas and Houston, and if the state's Latinos would just start voting at levels recently reached in California, Nevada, or Colorado, Texas might be able to emerge as a swing-vote state over the next few election cycles. Bird also took note of the vast amounts of money that wealthy Texas Democrats poured into national campaigns. Major candidates for president and the U.S. Senate and House always made one or more fund-raising trips through the state to haul in cash. But Bird also noticed that numerous Texas volunteers flocked to Obama's priority battleground states in 2008 and 2012, eager to help the Democrats win. He figured he could fund his efforts with Texas money and run it with Texas volunteers. Several wealthy Obama donors opened doors to key Texas Democrats, and Bird made the rounds to sell his story, raise his funds, and set up his Texas operation. Battleground Texas's appearance on the national stage gave many Democrats new hope that the effort would not only pump up dormant voter participation, but also help state senator Wendy Davis, fresh off of her 11-hour filibuster against abortion legislation, win her bid for governor.

But in the end, Battleground Texas failed miserably to turn Texas blue in 2014. Results for Davis, the Democratic candidate, were far worse than they had been in 2010, when Democrats thought they had a winner in Houston mayor Bill White, who also lost his race for governor. So while many political insiders and big-time consultants know that Texas matters in the overall scheme of things, and that Texas has the potential to shift the calculus in national elections, none of them has quite figured out how to do it. Turning Texas blue is not just about the numbers.

Few people really "get" Texas. We are too damn big. Too diverse. Too rich. Too poor. Contradictions abound.

We've got mountains, forests and deserts, and tornadoes, droughts and floods. Of course, everyone knows we've got all those oil rigs, but we've also got huge West Texas turbine farms that produce more wind power than any other state. We've got a 1,200-mile border with Mexico and have the world's twelfth-largest economy, with more exports than California and New York combined. We are more urban than rural, with three cities among the top ten largest in the country—Houston, Dallas, and San Antonio.

Yes, we have our racists and rabid gun nuts. We also have the nation's largest prison population and conduct more executions than most countries—while at the same time we have exonerated more DNA-cleared death-row inmates than anywhere in the world. These sordid statistics grab people's attention. There's just not much chatter about our brilliant theologians, world-class opera companies, top-rated cancer research centers, country music icons, writers, artists, top-flight movie producers, tech moguls—not to mention Heisman Trophy, Academy Award, and Pulitzer Prize winners, and Nobel laureates, too.

Those achievements and accolades are not what the country's most sophisticated political consultants and pundits see. To them, we're just a bunch of bumpkins who can't get our act together. Other states have their own homegrown political crazies, but ours

seem to outdo them all. Texas politics and policy has been com-
pletely captured by right-wing crackpots and overzealous Christian crusaders, and we haven't been able to stop them.

Anyone who wants to put Texas back in play nationally, or
make the Democratic Party matter again here, has to understand
how the state became such a hotbed of crazies and cranks in the
first place.

My years away from the game have helped me grapple more realistically with the larger trends that have shaped Texas today. After
Ann Richards fell to George W. Bush in 1994, I escaped into aca-
demia, wrote a few books, and ended up isolated in a liberal utopia
when I became CEO of KLRU-TV, Austin's PBS station. Being
stranded on the sidelines while Texas turned crazy was not very sat-
isfying for an old political junkie like me. I really wanted to figure
out what was going on and why. The funny thing is, once I started
to look at Texas's past and present with a strong dose of reality—as
well as a tiny bit of imagination—I could begin to view our recent
political history and raw culture without my usual liberal judgment.
By clearing away my biases, my wizened old eyes could actually see
a sort of path to bring about political change in Texas.

The writer Gertrude Stein once based a lecture on the notion
of "contemporariness": the idea that we rarely see our contemporary reality because we are so deeply embedded within it.[3] Stein
thought that in order to see the truth of "now" and to look at the
future with clear eyes, one had to be unencumbered by the pull of
the present. And she believed that it took an older generation, free
of the burden of contemporariness, to do that. That's me. Older.
Not exactly contemporary anymore, but not exactly living in the

past, either. I am acutely aware, however, that what happened long ago when Texas first turned red has a direct bearing on what is happening today and what might occur in the future.

So, this is a story of the past *and* the future, with the crazy present included. I see it through the lens of my own experience. How can I not?

I am a child of Texas, raised by Democratic parents who would rather have voted for a yellow dog than a Republican.[4] I married San Antonio journalist John Rogers, who became a master Democratic strategist for organized labor and trial lawyers during Texas's progressive heyday in the 1970s and '80s. We dragged our young children to rallies, parades, conventions, tedious meetings, and probably overdosed them with our dinner-table political chitchat. We were so deeply rooted in Texas politics that we each put countless hours into campaigns for candidates we believed in. John's untimely death at a young age after a four-year battle with cancer cut all of that short.

What I've learned from my own personal history, and Texas history in general, is that nothing is ever permanent. Change is always around the corner. In politics, change usually occurs when those in power grossly overextend themselves. Republicans have held power so long in Texas that they have become as sloppy, overconfident, and arrogant as Democrats used to be. But there are other factors pushing change as well, and some of them are actually beginning to cause a few leaks in their big red bubble.

Is there still a glimmer of hope for Texas Democrats after the complete drubbing they took along with Democrats in the rest of the nation in 2014? I think so, as long as we learn the lessons from the past. First, let's take a hard look at the disastrous 2014 Texas governor's race, figure out what happened—and why. Then let's tackle the most important question: Will Democrats ever be able to break the GOP grip on America's reddest state?

Yes, we can.

How? That's what we're about to figure out.

ONE

Reality of Defeat– One More Time

THE FIRST HINT THAT SOMETHING WAS AMISS came early—at a high-dollar fund-raiser at the $27 million, art-filled Dallas home of Naomi Aberly.

A Phi Beta Kappa graduate of Amherst College and the wife of hedge fund manager Larry Lebowitz, Aberly, in her early 40s, had been one the original Obama "bundlers" in 2008, and she raised more than $1 million for him in 2012. The president had even visited the Aberly-Lebowitz home twice for various events to raise money in Texas. After 2008, Aberly became a fixture in Democratic money circles in Texas. She was always generous and willing to help with dollars and hospitality, not only in politics but also in a variety of nonprofit causes—particularly for Planned Parenthood. She was one of Wendy Davis's earliest supporters and most influential advisors.

In early October 2013, shortly after Davis's formal announcement of her bid for governor, Aberly hosted the first big fund-raising event for her in Dallas, with ticket prices from $500 to $25,000. If you gave at the highest level, you could have dinner with Davis after the cocktail reception. More than 200 people filled Aberly's two-story atrium in the only home that famed architect Philip Johnson had ever designed in Dallas. Aberly had restored the 1964 contemporary mansion after it had fallen into disrepair, and she highlighted the magnificent dual staircases that led from the atrium to the upstairs private family quarters. With its elegant open spaces suitable for entertaining, the house was ideal for the kinds of fund-raising events Aberly enjoyed hosting.

The excitement in the air was palpable that fall evening. For many of Dallas's wealthy Democrats, this would be their first chance to meet the heroic and glamorous Wendy Davis, whose June 25, 2013, 11-hour filibuster against massive restrictions on abortion in the state had made her a national celebrity. Yet longtime Democratic Party fund-raiser Pat Pangburn heard something that evening that troubled her.

Aberly announced that the $200,000 raised at the event would be split 50–50 between the Davis campaign and something called the Texas Victory Fund, which would help pay for Battleground Texas's field operation to turn out new voters.

"What's this?" she whispered to a friend. "I want the money I raise to go directly to Wendy."[1]

Pangburn, who was on Davis's campaign finance committee, had never heard of the Texas Victory Fund, although she and almost everyone present were aware that Battleground Texas, founded by some of the wizards behind Obama's presidential campaign, had set up shop in Texas. Several months earlier, with great fanfare, they had announced that they were going to build an operation to turn Texas blue for the 2016 presidential election. Wendy Davis's gubernatorial campaign would be the perfect testing ground for their tactics.

"I thought Battleground was supposed to bring money into Texas," Pangburn said, "not take it out." That had been the impression earlier when Jeremy Bird, the Obama campaign field director in 2012, first came to Texas. He promised that he could activate a turnout surge of Hispanic voters, galvanize a youth vote, and develop the kind of grassroots organizational effort that Texas Democrats had never been able to carry off before.

Pangburn had been giving money to and fund-raising for Democrats since the 1970s. She had served on the Democratic National Committee, and had been an active supporter of Hillary Clinton's unsuccessful pursuit of the presidential nomination in 2008. In her private and professional life, Pangburn had raised horses as well as two children, and she had served as chair of the Texas Racing Commission when Ann Richards was governor. Pangburn's singular strength, however, was that she usually brought a healthy skepticism to political ventures. From the beginning she had wondered if the Battleground Texas organizers knew anything about the state's unique challenges or how to do what they promised. Now, she clearly did not like was she was hearing about how Wendy Davis's money would be split with the group. Why would any campaign give away half of the money it raised?

What Pangburn and other rich Democrats assembled in Aberly's home that evening did not know was that Battleground Texas and the Wendy Davis campaign had forged an unprecedented agreement to be equal partners in the race for Texas governor. The deal had been made some two months earlier. Several key Texas donors had been impressed with the massive get-out-the-vote (GOTV) field program Jeremy Bird had run for the Obama campaign in swing states like Ohio, Colorado, and Florida. They believed that the only way that Wendy Davis might win would be to use the Obama field campaign model. Even if she lost, they wanted to be sure that a strong organizational structure created by Battleground Texas would remain in place for 2016.

Steve and Amber Mostyn were first and foremost among the donors who believed that Battleground Texas could help Wendy Davis become governor. A true power couple in every sense of the word, the Mostyns were among the nation's top twenty-five national Democratic donors in 2012, by all accounts contributing more than $6 million to various Democratic super PACs. Amber Mostyn individually gave another $1 million to support women candidates, plus at least another $200,000 to Planned Parenthood's PAC.[2] For almost ten years the Mostyns had poured money into various Texas campaigns, and while often successful in their choices in various local races, they kept losing in the big statewide contests. They were ready for something new.

Trial lawyer Steve Mostyn, still in his 40s, had made a fortune suing insurance companies to help hurricane victims recover from severe property losses after massive natural disasters. In 2008, he made his reputation nationally after Hurricane Ike ripped through the Gulf of Mexico, causing $25 billion in damages and almost destroying Galveston Island. His later work with East Coast victims of Hurricane Sandy in 2012 brought him favorable coverage on CBS's *60 Minutes*, and even more money. Amber Mostyn, also a lawyer, kept up a busy practice while raising their young daughter, and she was heavily involved in recruiting and supporting pro-choice female candidates for the state legislature and other local races. Through these efforts she had become close friends with state senator Wendy Davis. Mostyn never hesitated to tell others that she wanted Wendy to be her governor.[3]

Jeremy Bird had obviously wowed the Mostyns with his big plans for Texas. Besides, after Obama's decisive victory in 2012, Bird had become the "cool campaign dude of the season," according to one top political consultant deeply involved in national campaigns.

What the Texas funders didn't realize was that Bird's approach to Texas was purely tactical rather than strategic. It was more about the techniques of voter registration and volunteer recruitment than about a comprehensive strategy to reach the kinds of voters that would matter to Democrats in a non-presidential election year. Savvy politicos know that a GOTV operation can add only a few percentage points to a close political campaign, and almost none at all if there is not a coherent strategy or a relevant message delivered by an inspiring candidate. Neither the key donors nor Davis herself seemed to understand the difference between tactics and strategy. While tactics were Jeremy Bird's strength, strategy was not. By the time Bird took over as national field director for the Obama campaign in 2012, the plan had already been written and was part of an integrated Electoral College–focused vote strategy developed at the highest levels of the campaign and not by Bird.[4] Because the Obama campaign would end up having almost $1 billion to spend, top campaign strategists David Axelrod and David Plouffe gave Bird room to experiment with various models of direct voter contact, and Bird excelled in reaching the voters he was directed to target. Yet his work was always within the parameters of the overall strategy. That was an important point that Texas donors missed when they insisted to Wendy Davis that Bird's operation would provide the path to victory. The fact that Davis herself didn't seem to have a clue about what she needed to do to, aside from securing the big money these donors promised her, made her willing to split money and decision making with Bird's operation.

While few people knew about this unique agreement at the time, Pat Pangburn recognized instinctively that fund-raising was going to be tough for Davis, despite all of the enthusiasm in the room that night. Pangburn decided that she would temper some of her initial enthusiasm and see what this Battleground Texas group and the Texas Victory Committee might actually do before she committed another dime to the effort. As it turned out, Pangburn's skepticism was warranted. Yet she remained marginally involved in the campaign effort and was close enough to see the snowballing disaster unfold and shatter hopes that 2014 would be a turning point for Democrats.

So Close and Still So Far

In the beginning Wendy Davis seemed to have it just right. She was fashionable and attractive, slim and leggy with flowing blonde hair—and smart to boot. In 1999, while practicing law and still a nominal Republican, she had gotten herself elected in a nonpartisan race for the Fort Worth City Council. There she built an alliance with developers to help to turn the booming Cowtown— where the West begins—into a sophisticated urban metropolis.

Wendy Davis loved both the politics and the policymaking aspects of public office, and a few years later, against all odds, she got herself elected to the Texas state senate. This time she ran as a Democrat and defeated popular Republican incumbent Kim Brimer. Davis's personal story resonated with women—even Republicans—and it was women who put her over the top in her GOP-leaning district. She had been a single mom, living in a trailer with her baby daughter, but she worked two jobs, attended night classes at the community college, earned a degree from Texas Christian University (TCU), and eventually became an honors graduate of Harvard Law School. It was an amazing story for a poor girl raised by a single mother who couldn't always put food on the table for her children. It was the kind of story Texans loved—proof that hard work could bring success to anyone.

In the Texas Senate, Davis got along well with both the Republican leadership and her Democratic colleagues, who were in a minority in the 31-member body. Early on, Davis emerged as a champion of public education and an advocate for women. She fought draconian cuts in public education and secured money to examine thousands of untested rape kits stacked in police evidence rooms to find DNA traces in crimes that had never been solved.

Then, on a summer night in June 2013, Wendy Davis became a star.

Wendy Davis electrified Texas—and the nation—with an 11-hour filibuster against one of the most restrictive anti-abortion laws proposed in Texas or any other state. Within hours almost 5,000 people filled the Capitol Rotunda in Austin late at night to cheer her on, and women all over the county were alerted on Twitter to listen to the live-stream broadcast coming from the senate floor. Although the filibuster failed to block the legislation, it did slow it down. Overnight, Davis had almost 70,000 followers on her Facebook page, and the clamor began for this remarkable woman to follow in Ann Richards's footsteps and run for governor. Her stand-alone filibuster, her courage and stamina, coupled with her inspiring personal story, triggered the liberal dream that Democrats might regain power after their 20-year miserable sojourn in the political wilderness of Red Texas.

Wendy Davis was "it."

And then she wasn't.

Over the course of a year, Wendy Davis emerged as the most reviled Democratic candidate in the sea of Democratic losses in 2014. The impact of the campaign's original hype and hubris quickly dissolved into the humiliation and hopelessness of its loss.

What happened?

She had raised over $30 million, some $8 million of which came from small individual donations on her website. Almost 20,000 volunteers flocked to her campaign. She had the paid advice of numerous political pros who had been part of Obama's heralded victory team. She had a staff of more than 150 people. She had a cover story in the *New York Times Magazine,* a *Vogue* fashion shoot, and became a regular presence on MSNBC. Her Republican opponent, Greg Abbott, was something of a right-wing nebbish whose claim to fame was that as Texas attorney general he went to the office every day looking for lawsuits to file against the Obama administration, which he did at least 30 times.

How did such blue promise turn into the worst Democratic failure in almost 20 years?

Davis lost, with 39 percent of the vote to Abbott's 59 percent, a loss far worse than former Houston mayor Bill White's 13 percent loss to Rick Perry back in 2010.

She lost 75 percent of the white vote.

She lost 54 percent of the women's vote, which her campaign had counted on to put her over the top.

She lost 44 percent of the Latino vote, a major base for the Democratic Party.

She lost in three of the six big cities that Democrats had counted on winning because of their strong base of African American and Hispanic voters.

In small cities, she got barely 10 percent of the white vote. And in one of the sparsely populated counties that make up the vast landmass of rural Texas, Davis received only one vote out of 99 cast for the Republican.

Democrats in every part of the state—those who had enthusiastically supported Davis from the beginning and those, like Pat Pangburn, who had stifled their skepticism to help her—spent the next three months venting their anger against all those operatives who had promised such sweet success. The blame game had begun.

The Davis Dilemma

When something goes terribly wrong, as it did in the Wendy Davis campaign for governor, there is sometimes a perverse, cruel glee that is produced in the aftermath, by friends and foes alike. As Ann Richards used to say, "They think you are a genius the day after you win, but they'll turn on you and call you an idiot the day after you lose." Very little in recent Texas politics matched the vitriol that hit poor Wendy Davis.

Texas Monthly put a gross caricature of Davis on its December 2014 cover, with a horrible distorted grimace on her face, her ample breasts spilling out of her low-cut dress, and her famous pink running shoes—which she'd donned for her marathon filibuster—dripping in disgusting brown cow dung. Oh well, it *is* Texas.

Was Davis a victim, a villain, or an innocent bystander in a campaign that was out of control from the beginning?

In 2013, the campaign began in chaos that was not of its own making and had the bad luck to emerge during one of the worst nationwide Democratic debacles in years. Still, if you can't fashion a strategy to lead you out of internal chaos or wage a focused campaign aimed at the kinds of Texas voters who are likely to vote in a non-presidential election year, then maybe you deserve to lose. On that basis alone, the Davis campaign warrants a serious critique.

After the June filibuster, Davis and her small state senate staff were simply overwhelmed by the outpouring of support, money, messages, pleas for public appearances, and national media interviews. Because donations began coming in on her website, they quickly set up a special campaign committee to receive the funds. But they were unprepared for what came next. Within days of the filibuster Planned Parenthood staged a huge rally for Davis on the Texas Capitol grounds and, like many other national groups, began to cite Davis's courage and leadership as a tool to raise money for their own organization. Groups from all over the country clamored for Davis's visits, or at least her name, to lend support to their own campaigns. She quickly became a marketing commodity for others who wanted to cash in on her celebrity. Davis was so flattered by the attention that she flitted all across the country, making speeches and appearing at fund-raisers for liberal groups or Democratic candidates. The time might have been better spent developing a game plan for an upcoming campaign.

The Fort Worth–based group of advisors who had helped Davis win her local races had never been involved in a statewide campaign before and were unsure about how to proceed. They were even undecided about whether she ought to use her newfound fame to bolster her bid for what looked like a difficult reelection campaign or to heed pleas from Democrats from all over the state to run for governor. Heady from the acclaim and instant stardom, Davis herself made the decision to run. The campaign began without a comprehensive strategy or even a campaign manager. Most of the critical early actions were left to a committee of Davis's friends. And the early decision to give up control over her campaign's field program to Battleground Texas set in motion a pattern of internal confusion that escalated into conflict when the campaign moved into high gear.

The problems for Wendy Davis began early and never ended.

Within a few weeks of the announcement of her run for governor, right-wing blogger Erick Erickson dubbed her "Abortion Barbie." Although the phrase ended up being a marvelous fund-raising tool for Davis that brought in hundreds of thousands of dollars from pro-choice women across the nation, it tainted her reputation among swing voters who viewed her as the single-issue candidate she said she did not want to be.

Even more damaging was a *Dallas Morning News* article that found glaring errors in Davis's heroic personal story: she had lived in a trailer for only a couple of months; her absent father had become a noted and respected theatrical producer in Fort Worth; and her wealthy second husband, with whom she had another child, helped put her through TCU and Harvard Law. After their divorce, he retained primary custody of their young daughter.[5]

You cannot run on biography if the biography is flawed or if important information is omitted. So from the get-go the Davis campaign gave Republican Greg Abbott plenty of ammunition to attack her. Because he had been planning to run for governor for a year, he started with more than $21 million in the bank and almost tripled that amount during the campaign. Davis was not without resources or opportunities herself, except neither she nor her advisors seemed to know how to use them.

Unfortunately, there were a few silly errors in personal judgment as well. Early in the campaign Joe Armstrong, a former publisher of *Rolling Stone* and nine other magazines, including *New York, New West,* and *Saveur,* had offered to squire Davis around New York to meet key people in media, as well as other potential high-dollar donors. An affable Texan with an army of friends both at home and in New York, Armstrong had been especially close to Ann Richards and had helped open doors to the rich and famous in New York for her campaigns. The unassuming Texan thought he might be able to help Davis in the same way. He entertained his friends so often that he became known as the "Mayor of Michael's," the renowned restaurant on 55th Street that was a regular gathering spot for television and publishing executives. He offered to set up a lunch there for Davis, but she was distracted and blew off one of the dates he had suggested for a brief getaway with her then-boyfriend. The lost opportunity infuriated Pat Pangburn, who saw it as one more indication of how difficult it was going to be to raise the kinds of dollars needed to carry the weight of the growing campaign staff and the enormous expenditures already taking place.

The root of these problems was that there was never a clear directive about priorities in scheduling, budgeting, or building a workable management structure. The internal confusion continued even after the president of Washington-based Emily's List, Stephanie Schriock, suggested that Karin Johanson be hired as campaign manager.

Johanson had an impressive record, having managed a number of high-profile campaigns, including the surprising victory of Tammy Baldwin, from Wisconsin, to the U.S. Senate in 2012. But Wisconsin is a small state compared with Texas, and Johanson never seemed to grasp the reality of the state—its size, complexities, diversity, political history, or the roles that various interest groups have traditionally played in Texas politics. Johanson's approach to the campaign seemed limited to presiding over regular conference calls with the bevy of campaign consultants she hired, including Obama pollster Joel Benenson, who was also handling Mark Udall's polling in Colorado.[6]

The phone calls among staff and consultants were often contentious, but Johanson tended to postpone key decisions until the consultants came to a consensus. She seemed intimidated by Battleground Texas and was unable to rein in the group's tendency to take independent actions unknown and unreported to the campaign. The bifurcated campaign structure resulted in the duplication of essential staff functions. Battleground had a full-blown press operation. So did the Davis campaign. Battleground had a digital operation, as did the Davis campaign. Battleground had a fund-raising apparatus. So did the Davis campaign. Confusion and conflict ensued, and Johanson never got a handle on the escalating tension between the two groups. Battleground provided reports on its field activities to the Davis campaign, but they were irregular, lacked vital information, and were rarely analyzed for meaning or accountability.

Spending was out of control as well. There were too many people and too few internal controls. Before Johanson came into the campaign, the overall budget was in the $40 million range. She immediately raised it to $60 million. There was little indication that donations were coming in fast enough to fund expenditures at that level, yet the campaign continued to spend as if the money was already in the bank.

The internal problems were mounting, and by the summer of 2014, when the campaign should have been in high gear, Karin Johanson and Wendy Davis were barely talking to each other. Many staff members were relieved when they came to a mutual parting of the ways. But what were they to do now?

For weeks, there was no management of the campaign, effective or otherwise. Davis finally persuaded her longtime friend Chris Turner to see if he could shape up the campaign for the final stretch.

Turner was one of the most promising young Democrats elected to the Texas legislature in recent years. He had twice defeated strong Republican candidates to win his suburban Fort Worth district, one of the few swing districts in the state. Turner's wife, Lisa, was an experienced veteran of many successful Texas campaigns and had become friends with Wendy when she helped get Wendy elected to the state senate. By the time Chris Turner came into the Davis campaign in midsummer, it was so late in the game that he could do little to bring order out of the chaos. Only about $25 million had been raised at that point, and half was already gone. The gossip machine among Texas politicos was already firing on all cylinders because it looked like the campaign was going nowhere. Reporters covering the campaign had been shooting darts for months because they felt mistreated by the campaign's disorganized press operation. To keep the faltering campaign alive, Turner had little choice except to slash key items in Karin Johanson's inflated campaign budget. "I had to cut all of our direct mail, as well as the TV buys in small markets," Turner said. "We just didn't have the money."[7] The funds that should have been budgeted for key expenditures during the last month of the campaign had already been spent—mainly on the huge staffs maintained by both Battleground and the Davis campaign.

In August, Turner rushed to Washington to try to raise $10 million from supportive labor unions and Democratic organizations to buy major-market TV time for the final two months of the campaign. He could rustle up only about $800,000. As a result, the campaign had a meager, ineffective TV ad buy and was unable to drop a single piece of direct mail to persuade swing voters, or motivate African American and Latino Democrats, or even let hard-core Democratic voters know where they could vote on Election Day—a staple of effective GOTV campaigns.

The results showed on Election Day. Voter turnout was abysmal, and the final numbers so devastating that it looked like Texas Democrats from top to bottom had simply been sucked into a black hole. One more time!

TWO

Lessons of 2014

THE EXTENT OF WENDY DAVIS'S 20-POINT loss may have been a surprise to campaign insiders, but it was a total shock to her donors and volunteers. Many had been led to believe that pollster Joel Benenson's numbers were showing only about a seven-to-nine point disadvantage going into the final weeks of the campaign. Only a handful of astute observers who understood the Texas electorate and had not been involved in the campaign were predicting a double-digit wipeout. Few people believed them. Insiders describe Benenson as visibly shaken on election night as the results were tallied. Of course another of his top clients, Colorado Senator Mark Udall, was also losing his race.

In the weeks following the election, amid the despair and depression, Democrats struggled to look ahead to "next time." Would they keep making the same old mistakes or would they take the time to learn a few lessons from 2014? If you made a case study about what *not* to do in a statewide Texas political campaign in the future, you could find everything you need to know within the Wendy Davis campaign.

- *Lesson One.* The campaign made an erroneous assumption that the surge of enthusiasm among women because of the abortion filibuster would extend beyond Austin and galvanize suburban women to vote for Davis. That did not happen. There were other, equally troubling assumptions, among them that Hispanic voters would automatically vote Democratic and that voter turnout would be higher in 2014 than in 2010, the previous non-presidential election year. None of that was true. *Successful ventures take the time to test their assumptions against facts and data and rarely venture out without assessing the reality of current conditions.*
- *Lesson Two.* The campaign never had a written plan or week-by-week playbook to guide its efforts. When Chris Turner became manager toward the end of the campaign, he asked to see a copy of the game plan and was handed a two-page memo that outlined broad goals but provided no specific strategy or time frame to reach them. *Successful ventures always have a detailed plan of action with benchmarks along the way that follow an overall strategy and budget.*
- *Lesson Three.* The campaign got trapped in the predicament of taking actions that were either too early or too late. The decision to enter the governor's race was made in emotional haste without taking the time to weigh the consequences. Once the campaign was up and running, however, key decisions got caught up in bureaucratic wrangling between the campaign staff and Battleground Texas that often took

days to resolve. It took more than a week for the campaign to refute the unfavorable *Dallas Morning News* article about Davis's personal life. *Successful ventures are flexible enough to move quickly and shift course in response to changing circumstances.*

- *Lesson Four.* There was an appalling failure to ask critical questions about the Texas electorate or the cultural implications of shifting demographics. Would Hispanic Catholics actually vote for Abortion Barbie? Flashing red lights signaled trouble during the March 2014 Democratic primary. Even though she won overwhelmingly, Davis lost 20 South Texas counties with large Hispanic populations to an unknown Democrat with a Spanish surname. Could this be an indication of trouble ahead? The campaign seemed to shrug off the results without heeding the warning. *Successful ventures heed key warning signals along the way.*

- *Lesson Five.* The campaign never had a strategy to reach white voters. In their canvassing, Battleground Texas volunteers were supposed to classify voters into three categories: (1) off the table; (2) hard but persuadable; and (3) on board. If voters were Anglo, the assumption was that they were probably "off the table," meaning that they might be difficult to persuade to vote for Davis and probably not worth the time or effort to pursue. Even though Davis had always considered white, pro-choice women a likely source of voters, there was never a distinct strategy to win them to her cause. While Planned Parenthood's PAC spent $2.6 million to target identified pro-choice voters, the Davis campaign never developed an effective strategy to reach

Anglo women for whom abortion might not have been a primary issue. As a result, white voters were basically ignored. Given the fact that exit polling had shown that white voters in non-presidential election years still averaged 65 percent of the vote, how can you write off two-thirds of the voters and expect to win?[1] *Successful ventures do not ignore two-thirds of their potential audience.*

- *Lesson Six.* The campaign never developed an overarching issue encompassed in a succinct message to appeal to all voters. There was never a theme that defined Davis as an individual who could lead Texas to a better future. In 1990, Ann Richards used two big issues to demonstrate herself as a leader who could solve the state's problems. She pledged to establish a state lottery to erase a potential budget deficit, and she advocated insurance reform that would help every Texan who owned a car or a home. It didn't matter if voters were black, white, or Hispanic. The issues cut across race, ethnicity, and income levels and portrayed Richards as a dynamic leader who could bring about change. No message cut through the clutter from the Davis campaign except that Davis was for abortion and her opponent, Greg Abbott, was simply a bad guy. *Successful ventures have a defining message that informs people what they are all about.*

The mistake that most critics focused on, however, was Wendy Davis's decision to cede control of the campaign's ground game, voter targeting, and data collection to Battleground Texas. And the lesson here is clear: *Successful ventures do not give up control of their operations.*

If we don't heed the lessons from the Davis campaign, we will keep cooking from the same old recipe for disaster.

Battleground or Battle-Scam?

Battleground Texas at times seemed more like a vendor than a true partner with the Wendy Davis campaign. But it was a vendor without true accountability. One disgruntled Democrat started calling the operation "Battle-Scam."

The group ended up receiving about $6 million from Davis's Texas Victory Fund, the fund-raising vehicle shared with her campaign. It probably raised an additional $3 to $4 million on its own. But the Davis team rarely had access to the details of Battleground's fieldwork. Until Chris Turner came into the campaign, few campaign officials had even analyzed the details that Battleground did provide. It was only then that they realized the voter contact results were hugely inflated.

When Battleground claimed that volunteers had made 20,000 voter contacts in a single weekend, a close reading of the report revealed that dialing a wrong phone number was considered a voter contact. If a volunteer knocked on a door and no one answered, but the household contained four registered voters who lived at that address, Battleground volunteers counted the knock on the door as four voter contacts. These reports were the basis for early optimism that the campaign was reaching huge numbers of potential Davis voters. Yet the numbers provided little information that might be useful to assess actual voter support for Davis. Until about halfway through the campaign, few people understood what was actually involved in the fieldwork program.

The Amway Plan

Jeremy Bird and his Obama field team had developed an "Amway" or direct sales–style approach to recruit volunteers for the 2012 presidential campaign, and Battleground Texas imported that model. It was like a rolling pyramid scheme—except it would be built on volunteers instead of money or product sales. Paid organizers would recruit an initial set of volunteers, then train them to recruit other volunteers who would keep recruiting other volunteers, ad infinitum. The plan was to build the largest army of campaign volunteers that Texas had ever seen. Phone banks recruited volunteers. Door-to-door canvassers recruited volunteers. Neighborhood gatherings and labor union meetings recruited volunteers. And so did e-mail blasts to thousands of Democrats gleaned from one list or another. Battleground organizers claimed in press releases that over the course of the campaign, they had recruited some 34,000 volunteers. But what were they going to do with all of those people?

The plan was to have them conduct extensive voter registration drives to bring new voters into the process and then identify potential supporters for Davis among the registrants. When Texas's two-week early voting period started, volunteers would be marshaled to conduct the most massive get-out-the-vote (GOTV) effort Texas had ever seen. That was how Obama won Ohio and other states, or so key Davis donors and campaign staffers believed. If they had bothered to fully vet the process, they would have learned something quite different.[2]

As national field director of the 2012 Obama campaign, Jeremy Bird had indeed built an amazing volunteer field operation, claiming that some 22 million volunteers had transformed campaigning in America. And that was partly true. But what Texas donors and the Davis campaign missed was that the true geniuses of Obama's national campaign staff—David Axelrod and David Plouffe—had approved the targeting plan before Jeremy Bird was hired to implement it.[3] Bird's talent was in finding innovative ways to carry it out. The campaign had so much money at its disposal that it could afford to experiment with Bird's multifaceted efforts to implement the plan.

The reality of the Obama 2012 victory was that in crucial battleground states like Ohio, the bulk of the GOTV work was handled not only by volunteers but by paid canvassers, mainly from organized labor, who turned out key voters they knew would vote for Obama.

Jenn Brown, the energetic and talented young organizer whom Jeremy Bird put in charge of Battleground Texas while he tended to other campaign business across the country, had been Obama's field director in Ohio in 2012. Brown knew how to recruit and train volunteers and deploy them where the national campaign needed them to be, and she seemed to do an amazing job of recruiting volunteers in Texas in 2014. The problem was that she rarely knew where to send her volunteers to register likely new Democratic voters and failed to prioritize canvassing in neighborhoods that were critical to generating a big minority turnout. Unfortunately, her periodic reports failed to convey the kinds of critical information that could actually help the Davis campaign make key decisions. While Battleground's reports purported to show a massive field effort under way, that's not what Democratic activists in local communities were seeing. After Labor Day, complaints from

Democrats who usually ran GOTV operations in their areas began to flood the Davis campaign headquarters.

What were Battleground's troops doing registering voters in upscale Republican neighborhoods? Why weren't they canvassing in African American and Hispanic neighborhoods? Republican consultants actually claimed that when they followed up on the newly registered voters that Battleground claimed were Democrats, they found that almost half of them planned to vote Republican.[4]

The problem was that plans to identify minority Democratic "fall-off voters"—those who voted Democratic in presidential election years but almost always failed to show up in off-year elections—had fallen short. Because the massive volunteer recruitment effort had produced mostly white volunteers, there was also a serious shortage of people who actually canvassed the neighborhoods where many minority voters lived. All of this was masked in Battleground's glowing progress reports.

State senator Rodney Ellis, who represented a largely African American district in Houston, reported that he saw no signs of Battleground canvasses in black precincts. Congressman Mark Veasey, whose district includes large numbers of African American voters in the Fort Worth area, saw no activity in his district, either. The same was true in Houston's huge Hispanic community, which is second only to Los Angeles in raw numbers. "There was no evidence of any kind of Hispanic effort, and as a result the turnout was abysmal," according to Dr. Richard Murray, a political scientist who teaches at the University of Houston and polls regularly for Democratic candidates.[5] And officials in the heavily Latino Rio Grande Valley complained that Battleground organizers were not effective in their canvassing operations because they simply did not understand the communities in which they were working.

It wasn't until about two weeks before early voting started that Battleground's Jenn Brown notified the Davis campaign that it was unlikely that the promised voter turnout targets could be met. Still, after early voting began, Jeremy Bird put out a press release bragging that the early turnout numbers were higher than in previous off-year elections and that the Democratic vote totals would exceed all expectations. Davis's campaign manager, Chris Turner, who had begun checking numbers on his own and talking to Democrats all over the state, warned Bird that his numbers could be off.[6] Bird released the numbers anyway. It took only a day or so before members of the Texas news media did their own fact checking with local election officials and realized how inaccurate Bird had been. As a result, he had to sheepishly retract his report and claim he had simply used the wrong data set.

By then, local Democrats realized they were in serious trouble because of their reliance on Battleground. Begging and borrowing resources, the Davis campaign and political groups like the Texas Organizing Project, the Lone Star Project, organized labor, local party officials, and individual candidates began to put their own paid canvassers on the ground. The last-minute paid canvassing managed to save the Democratic vote in Dallas. But the push came too late, and they were too far behind to make a difference in Houston or San Antonio.

Post-election analysis of the Battleground effort was brutal. A careful review of Battleground's volunteer data revealed that many of the volunteers showed up to help only once or twice, with a much smaller number of activists who actually participated regularly in the overall operation. Battleground claimed that its 34,000 volunteers had registered over 97,000 new voters, but that averages to about three newly registered voters per volunteer—hardly a noteworthy effort to have consumed so much money and time.

Republicans, of course, were jubilant, pointing out how they had managed to snooker the Democrats and their Obama-trained saviors one more time. Local Democrats were almost as derisive as Republicans. As the state and national news media looked at detailed results and picked up Democratic complaints, the headlines told the story: "How Battleground Texas Hobbled the Wendy Davis Campaign"; "What Went Wrong with Battleground Texas"; "The Future of Battleground Texas"; and "Losing Ground," a particularly devastating story in the *Texas Observer*, the long-standing voice of Texas liberals.[7]

While it is highly unlikely that Davis—or any Texas Democrat—could have won in 2014 because of the national Republican sweep, a well-run campaign certainly could have narrowed the 20-point margin of the loss. The Wendy Davis campaign in 2014 should become an important reminder for smart Democrats about what they must do differently the next time around.

Did It Matter?

After all the fanfare about Battleground Texas, the effort turned out to be surprisingly irrelevant to the 2014 election results. Although in 2010 Democratic gubernatorial candidate Bill White had lost badly, in retrospect he ran a more effective campaign *without* Battleground Texas than the Wendy Davis campaign did with it. In 2014, the total voter turnout in Texas was only 4.7 million, a decline of about 5 percent from 2010. Only 33.4 percent of Texas's 14.2 million registered voters actually cast ballots, down from 38 percent in 2010. Battleground failed to pump the vote in any category, and because so many local campaigns relied on the group's direction for their local field programs, the effort left a wave of anger, regret, and resolve among many Texas Democrats. Never again would they trust Battleground Texas, or any outside organization like it, with the sole responsibility of turning Texas blue.

Former Galveston judge Susan Criss, who lost her Battleground-targeted "Blue Star" legislative race by 9 percentage points (54 to 45 percent), said she was initially flattered that Battleground had picked her race as a focus for their efforts. "I liked them, they seemed to be disciplined in their operation, and that's not always true of our Democrats," she recalled.[8]

Criss's district had consistently sent Democrats to the state legislature since the end of Reconstruction. But recent redistricting had shifted Galveston into swing-voter territory. Criss knew that to win, she needed to pull in crossover Republican voters as well as generate a heavy minority turnout. The 20-year veteran of Texas politics had the contacts and credentials to do so. When she saw that neither of those efforts was under way, she tried to convince Battleground's field operatives to redirect their attention to areas she felt were necessary to produce the votes she needed, but to no avail. "They were such true believers that they didn't want to make changes in their approach when it was obvious that it wasn't working. They believed what they believed and you couldn't get through to them," she said.

Jeremy Bird has heard all of this by now, and he has obviously been humbled by his Texas experience. "We made the wrong assumptions about the floor . . . we didn't believe we could get any lower than the 43 percent Bill White got in his governor's race in 2010," Bird said. "Realistically, we could only count on about 35 to 36 percent."[9]

That was a much steeper hill to climb than Battleground had envisioned, and it was one more erroneous assumption that sank a well-meaning Democratic rally.

As the memory of the 2014 election faded, only a few paid Battleground Texas staff members remained in the state through 2015, still recruiting volunteers, registering voters, and maintaining a digital database. Bird and key supporters remain convinced that they had created something permanent and important for the future of Texas—an updated voter contact file and a system for recruitment and training. Bird now says that he knew all along it would be a marathon, "a Texas-sized marathon . . . it was not going to be a one-cycle race."

Jeremy Bird was no scammer, as some critics charged. Nor were the bright young organizers he brought into Texas insincere about what they wanted to do. They worked hard. They put in long hours. They wanted to win. They simply ran an operation that was ill-conceived and ineffective to boot.

The disorganized Wendy Davis campaign cannot avoid responsibility for its own loss or blame it all on Battleground Texas. The campaign was seriously flawed from the beginning. And of course, the national Republican sweep that year created an atmosphere that probably doomed it all along.

But Texas itself was a factor. It is not an easy state to win when you start at the bottom with limited resources, limited imagination, a limited candidate, and a limited understanding of the electorate that actually votes in non-presidential elections. Even though organic demographic changes were already beginning to work to Democrats' advantage, neither the Davis campaign nor Battleground Texas understood how to use them. And so Texas Democrats racked up yet another loss with another seriously flawed campaign, just as they have for the past 20 years.

Candidates matter. Circumstances matter. Campaigns matter. They have to be about something that connects voters with the kind of future they would like to see. A successful campaign still has to be built around a leader who has a theme and a message and understands how to motivate the electorate.

Republicans in Texas learned that many years ago.

Republicans got several important things right in their 40-year trek to political power in Texas. They understood that Texas's most consistent voters in off-year state elections often exhibit a basic rawness and resentment of both taxes and government authority. Beginning in the 1980s, Republicans began to pick out the groups who might support their candidates—evangelical churchgoers, Reagan Democrats, white suburbanites, gun owners, residential property taxpayers, and small business entrepreneurs. They learned to take advantage of every mistake Democrats made—and there were plenty. Finally, Republicans owned the angry passion underdogs need to fuel their battles.

How Texas Republicans managed to do all of this was as much a matter of luck and circumstance as it was the sheer brilliance of their leaders. The question now is, can they sustain what they have created? The answer may be rooted in their very beginnings—before the crazies and crackpots took over their party. One important fact emerges: contrary to popular belief, the Republican Party of Texas did not begin with Karl Rove. The truth is both more interesting and much more complicated. And the story begins before Rove was even born.

THREE

Rise of the Outsiders

LAWYER TOM LUCE REPRESENTS WHAT THE best Texas Republicans used to be like—before Karl Rove, before Tom DeLay and Rick Perry and Ted Cruz. Although Republicans like Luce were rock-ribbed conservatives, they managed to be collegial and even cordial most of the time. Many held a belief, in an antiquated "good citizen" kind of way, that public service involved supporting public institutions as well as community charities. Their goal was not to destroy government but to make it work for business, banking, and oil. Many like Luce saw the value and necessity of tempering their public rhetoric. This was particularly true after the 1963 assassination of President John F. Kennedy in Dallas.

Bankers and business leaders who had run the town for decades decided they wanted no more of the extreme right-wing, anti-Communist hysteria that had gripped Dallas in the 1950s. Plain and simple, it had become bad for business. The hateful rhetoric of the John Birch Society, the racist rants on talk radio paid for by oilman H. L. Hunt, and the demonization of social justice–seeking pastors and professors had turned Dallas into a hotbed of radical right-wing activity that rarely worried the downtown business community—until after the assassination. Now, Dallas's reputation as a good place to do business and make money was at stake. The lid was on, and Republicans of Luce's stripe brought a more moderate approach that did not stir up hatred or venom or Communist conspiracy theories, at least in public.

Tom Luce's story is key to understanding the development of the modern GOP in Texas: the persistence of the men and women who built the party and those who have now watched it turn into a coterie of clowns, crackpots, and callous haters of government at any level.

The grandson of a yellow-dog Democrat from Kentucky who settled in Texas, Luce became a Republican in the early 1960s while in law school at Southern Methodist University. To him, it seemed like an "anti-establishment" kind of thing to do.

"I guess it sounds silly now to think that becoming a Republican would be anti-establishment, but the Democrats controlled everything, and I was looking for something new," Luce explained.[1]

He was on to something important, as were many ambitious young professionals. They wanted no part of the messy Democratic Party of Texas, which had been locked in internecine warfare for decades. Nearly a century of grievances, going all the way back to Reconstruction after the Civil War, were still being played out in power struggles among various factions within the ruling party.

The Texas Way

After federal troops left Texas in 1870 at the end of Reconstruction, many of the "Old Three Hundred," the original Anglo settlers who in the 1820s had received large land grants from Stephen F. Austin's first Texas colony, began to expand their fortunes in ranching, trade, and banking. Although many were barely touched by the destruction and economic devastation experienced in the states of the Deep South, the defeat of the Confederacy had left most white Texans, rich and poor, with a hatred of the federal government—or any government. The new 1876 Texas Constitution, written after the state was readmitted to the Union, was designed to severely limit the power of officials to act decisively—or quickly—on pressing issues, thus ensuring a fairly weak central government. Texas still operates under that timeworn document, although it has been amended almost 500 times.

As the wealth of individual Texans grew and stability returned to the state, it was not unusual for South Texas ranch and banking families to send their children east to school.[2] A certain Victorian gentility prevailed in their social circles, and they generally associated only with others like themselves, mostly ignoring the poor farmers, tradesmen, or Mexican laborers who crossed back and forth across the porous border to work on South Texas ranches. Even so, these laborers had it better than former slaves, who struggled to survive in the aftermath of the Civil War.

At the time blacks were hard to ignore because they made up about a third of Texas's 550,000 residents. They outnumbered whites in areas of deep East Texas, and many flocked to Houston looking for work and homes in the city's poorer neighborhoods. Their very existence as free men and women was an affront to many whites, who took widespread vengeance on them after federal troops left the state. As in other parts of the South, the Ku Klux Klan emerged to terrorize blacks and restore what some saw as the "natural order" of the races—whites on top, blacks on the bottom. By the turn of the new century African Americans had been so effectively segregated by Jim Crow laws and disenfranchised by the 1902 imposition of a poll tax that it would take 60 years and the enactment of civil rights legislation and federal court orders before they became a factor in Texas elections.

In 1900, when the great gushing oil wells at Spindletop, outside Beaumont, were producing up to 75,000 barrels of oil a day, what we think of as modern Texas began to emerge. Newly rich speculators and drillers scooped up land leases all over the state— sometimes finding oil but often coming up with dry holes. With the roughnecks who worked the big rigs, they brought a certain coarseness and raw greed and power hunger to Texas life, and it often spilled over into their politics. Hard work, hard lives, and hard liquor were staples of the new oil culture. The early oil boom era was so raucous that the state government finally had to step in, impose a few regulations, and bring order to the chaos in the fields.

Although many Texans grew rich from the oil boom, the ranching successes, the building of railroads, and the growth of shipping ports along the Gulf Coast, the state itself remained relatively poor.[3] Tenant farmers, Mexican laborers, and poor white itinerants who worked in the new refineries and on the docks saw little benefit from the new wealth. Of course, black laborers and field hands saw even less. Yet whether rich or poor, white

Texas men kept voting for Democrats out of Southern loyalty and tradition. They embodied what some have called the "Texas Way": a profound distrust of distant authority, a belief in Texas's uniqueness, and a penchant for personal autonomy that required a benign government to leave them alone. It was perfectly okay for the bankers, lawyers, and wealthy elite to run the government because it wouldn't make much difference anyway.[4] That's just the way it was. The oft-repeated tales of the state's heroic beginnings as a sovereign nation—with its martyrs who died at the Alamo and its ragtag fighters who defeated the superior Mexican army during the Battle of San Jacinto—took on a mythic quality and allowed ordinary Texans to see themselves as "special," with all the fervor of religious zealots. Simply being Texan seemed to endow most white farmers, laborers, oil-field workers, and city service providers with a feeling of superiority, almost as if they, too, were part of the ruling class by virtue of belonging to such a great nation-state.[5]

Texas's one-party Democratic state featured all of the recurring infighting, ambition, cronyism, and barely hidden corruption that occurs when one party or group holds power over long periods of time. Neither the occasional rumblings of disaffected whites nor those of disenfranchised blacks made much difference. The agrarian populist movement in the 1870s and '80s, which started with a farmers' alliance in Texas, had a far greater impact outside the state than within. The movement arose because of falling crop prices, high bank interest rates on farm loans, exorbitant railroad fees to ship crops, and restrictions on paper money in favor of gold— all of the elements that pitted small farmers against the powerful economic interests that dominated state government. While the early populists never achieved significant power in Texas, they did leave a residue of resentment toward politicians in Austin who favored the haves over the have-nots. The populists' ideas carried over into the twentieth century as the first visible rejections of the Texas Way.

It took women, however, to actually begin softening the hard-edge Texas Way. At the turn of the twentieth century, the state had active movements for prohibition and women's suffrage that propelled women into the political arena. In 1918 Texas women won the right to vote in state elections a full year before the 19th Amendment to the United States Constitution was ratified. These well-educated, progressive women, usually the wives or daughters of well-to-do men, were part of the early women's club movement that sprang up around the country. They brought the Carnegie-funded libraries to small towns throughout Texas, offering children of poor farmers and laborers access to books and learning—always a dangerous activity in an autocratic society.[6] As early as 1915 women got the Texas legislature to outlaw child labor, establish compulsory school attendance rules, and supply free textbooks for Texas school children. They even managed to elect the first woman to statewide office in 1918: Annie Webb Blanton, who became the superintendent of public education. Voters also chose women to serve in the Texas legislature and in scattered county offices. Although there were always grumblings about the changes these women and their progressive male allies wanted to make, they posed no real threat to those who held political and economic power. It took Franklin D. Roosevelt and the New Deal to do that.

The New Deal and Birth of the
Modern Republican Party

In the 1930s, to combat the devastation of the Great Depression, President Roosevelt imposed new regulations on banks and created big government relief and job programs to put Americans back to work. Some of Texas's wealthiest families, however, could not abide the new breed of Texas Democrats who found hope in the New Deal and wanted the federal government to do even more. They were further incensed in 1944 when the U.S. Supreme Court ruled that Texas's all-white Democratic primary was unconstitutional, forcing the party to allow blacks to vote in primary elections. Anti–New Deal Democrats, known as the "Texas Regulars," were so fed up with federal intervention into Texans' lives that they put out their own version of a party platform. It attacked every social and economic advance made by the Democrats to pull the nation out of the Great Depression. The platform was virulent in its anger and extremist in its language. It called for a return to states' rights that had been "destroyed by the Communist-controlled New Deal, and a restoration of the supremacy of the white race."[7]

The Texas Regulars and the New Dealers battled for control of the state's Democratic Party until 1948, when two events provided the catalysts that finally drove Texas Regulars out. One had to do with race and the other with power, the two dominant themes throughout modern Texas political history. First, President Harry S. Truman issued an executive order to end racial segregation in the armed services, which reinforced the worst fears of the archconservative segregationists about the "mongrelization" of the races.[8] But it was Lyndon B. Johnson's disputed victory in the 1948 Democratic primary for U.S. Senate that sent them packing.

Elected to the U.S. House of Representatives in 1937, Johnson was a protégé of President Roosevelt. He brought millions of federal dollars to Texas during the Depression and later to defense contractors during World War II. Having grown up in the hardscrabble Hill Country, he knew the benefits that federal programs like rural electrification could bring to the farmers who eked out a living there. Johnson secured money to establish a system of dams and lakes that provided water for rice farmers along the Gulf Coast and electrical power for Central Texas—including the state capital, in Austin. While Johnson had ties to the Texas oil industry, huge defense contractors, and other economic behemoths in the state, his support for President Roosevelt's big government projects had earned him fierce enemies among the deeply conservative, racist claque that controlled state government in Austin.

In the 1948 Senate primary, Johnson defeated the incumbent governor, Coke Stevenson, a die-hard Texas Regular. Johnson's famously slim victory margin amid charges of massive voter irregularities proved too much for Stevenson's supporters.[9] They claimed, but never proved, that Johnson had stolen the election because local officials in South Texas packed the ballot boxes with names of nonexistent voters. When those late-arriving South Texas boxes were tallied, Johnson overcame a 20,000-vote deficit in early results and won by only 87 votes out of almost 1 million cast. From that time on, Johnson was known in some circles as "Landslide Lyndon." For years, Texas Regulars had toyed with leaving the Democratic Party, and Stevenson's defeat gave them as good a reason to bolt as any. They switched their loyalty, money, and votes to the Republican Party.

Although presidential elections always drew a small scattering of Republican votes after Reconstruction, there was really no effective or functional Republican Party structure until the Texas Regulars came on the scene. These newly minted Republicans were from the wealthiest families in the state, and they quickly rose to power in the national party. Houston's Oveta Culp Hobby, the publisher of the *Houston Post*, held a cabinet post in the Dwight D. Eisenhower administration, and Anne Armstrong—who with her husband, Tobin, owned one of the largest ranches in South Texas—became an advisor to Richard M. Nixon and, later, Gerald R. Ford's ambassador to Great Britain. Although there was now an official Republican Party in Texas, with a structure and set of committees, the founders were such an elite, exclusive group that they focused almost entirely on national politics and spent little time expanding their base in Texas. They never abandoned the Democratic Party at the local level, either. They would cast their votes for the most conservative candidates in Democratic primaries and then turn around and vote for the Republicans in the general elections.

Even without the presence of some of the state's wealthiest and most influential families, the turf battles within the Democratic Party raged on, and race, power, and oil still set the terms.

Liberals on the Horizon

In 1952 and 1956, the most conservative elements of the Democratic Party were now identified in Texas's unique parlance as

"Shivercrats" because they had coalesced around three-term Democratic governor Allen Shivers, who jumped to the Republicans' aid in the 1952 presidential election. Shivers supported Eisenhower, a Republican war hero, over liberal Democrat Adlai Stevenson because Eisenhower pledged to allow Texas control of its tidelands, the underwater land that extends ten miles into the Gulf of Mexico. It was an archaic dispute with the federal government arising from Texas's unique history as an independent nation. Texas claimed that it entered the Union with territory extending ten miles into the Gulf of Mexico; the federal government insisted that Texas conform to the same three-mile offshore boundary that applied to other coastal states. The dispute had smoldered for decades and took on new importance when oil companies wanted to drill in the tidelands without having to comply with federal oversight. Although the matter was complicated, confusing, and of little interest to ordinary Texans, Governor Shivers's demagoguery turned the issue into one of those states-rights tirades that reflected the Texas Way and resided deep in some recesses of the Texas psyche. Shivers was able to lead conservative-leaning Democrats into the Republican presidential column for the first time since Reconstruction.

Now it was the New Deal Democrats' turn to be incensed. After the 1952 election, the liberal-loyalist wing of the party began serious organizing against the Democrat-turned-Republican Shivercrats, and Judge Ralph Yarborough emerged as standard-bearer for the liberals. He ran a strong race against Shivers in 1954, coming close to defeating him. As one Texas liberal gloated, even in defeat, "We scared the bejesus out of the old guard and we were never going to be frozen out again."[10]

For the first time the emerging labor unions, populist farmers, loyal New Deal Democrats, and an increasingly active NAACP—which by 1943 already had more than 6,000 members in Houston alone—began to show some strength on Election Day. Mexican Americans, too, flexed their political muscle after a group of Latino veterans of World War II created the American G.I. Forum and began calling attention to Texas's continuing discrimination against Mexican Americans in the public schools, residential neighborhoods, and in the delivery of public services. They were also running for office, winning local elections in South Texas and San Antonio. Henry B. Gonzalez became the first Mexican American to serve on the San Antonio City Council, and in 1956 he became the first Mexican American to be elected to the state senate. The goals of this growing progressive movement were amplified by a new, independent biweekly journal, *The Texas Observer*, edited by Ronnie Dugger and funded almost entirely by Mrs. Frankie Randolph, a wealthy liberal Democrat from Houston. The liberal coalition now had a voice to articulate their needs, as well as a statewide leader in Yarborough. And he had a populist flair and zealous determination to shine a light on the poor services and favors to the rich provided by their state government.

Lyndon Johnson recognized the growing power of the liberal movement at home, and he was ready to use it to rid Texas's Democratic Party of the troublesome Shivercrats.

After his election to the U.S. Senate, Johnson became the most powerful politician in Texas, amassing a notable following among the state's most ambitious young lawyers and business leaders who would shape state and national policy for years to come.[11] Johnson's accumulation of political and economic power in Texas was enhanced by his concomitant rise to power in Washington, D.C. As Senate majority leader, he became a master of persuasion and punishment, and with the help of the old Southern mossbacks who chaired the major committees, he ruled the Senate with an iron fist. By the late 1950s, he began to envision himself as president of the United States, but to be a contender for the nomination in 1960, he needed to make himself more acceptable to liberals within the national Democratic Party. So in 1956, Johnson joined with the Yarborough forces to run the Shivers crowd and the segregationist Dixiecrats out of the party.

Although I didn't realize the significance of the event at the time or the power at stake for Lyndon Johnson, it was my own experience at the state Democratic Party convention, where the Johnson and Shivers forces clashed, that led me into the stormy world of Texas politics. My parents were followers of the liberal Yarborough, who controlled about a third of the delegates at the convention. Although I was a young teenager, they let me tag along to watch the showdown everyone knew was coming. The passion and excitement of the convention—the intrigue, plots, and even the brawls—drew me in like a magnet. From then on, I wanted to be in the middle of it. The Johnson-Yarborough forces won the day, and I was fascinated by the competition and camaraderie that politics could bring when focused on causes that really mattered to people. Driving hard-core segregationists out of the Democratic Party was a cause worth fighting for—even for a naïve young kid like me.

Still, even after their joint success at the state convention, there was no love between the Johnson and Yarborough factions. In 1957, U.S. Senator Price Daniel resigned his seat to return to

Texas to make a run for governor, and a special election was held to fill the Senate vacancy. To the surprise and consternation of conservatives, Ralph Yarborough managed to win the special election over Lyndon Johnson's handpicked candidate. Texas liberals were euphoric, but their victory only intensified the open warfare within the Democratic Party.

Sudden Opening

In the continuing melee between powerful Johnson Democrats and the shaky coalition of Yarborough liberals, there seemed to be no opportunity for ambitious young conservatives like Tom Luce.

Then, in 1960, there was a sudden opening for the Republicans—an unexpected gift from Lyndon Johnson. When the Democratic presidential nominee, John F. Kennedy, selected him to be his running mate, Johnson's friends in the Texas legislature arranged for him to also run for reelection to his U.S. Senate seat at the same time. The move would ensure that Johnson could still hold his Senate seat if the Democratic ticket lost the presidential election. Republicans were incensed by the cronyism of Johnson's dual campaign, and John Tower, a 35-year-old unknown Republican college professor from Wichita Falls in northwest Texas, decided to run against Johnson for his Senate seat.

Young lawyer Tom Luce saw his opportunity to act against the establishment and began volunteering for John Tower, whose supporters fanned out across the state, campaigning in every nook and cranny as no Republican had ever done before. Even though he lost to Johnson, Tower drew almost a million votes—unprecedented for a Republican in Texas. And although the Kennedy-Johnson ticket carried the state, Richard Nixon got an astounding 49 percent of the Texas vote. It was enough to encourage Tower to run for Johnson's now-vacant Senate seat in a special election in 1961. A few months later, the sole Republican in a field of 71 candidates, John Tower managed to forge a victory and become the first Republican elected to statewide office in 90 years.

Tower's election inspired a new generation of antiestablishment, conservative Republicans who profoundly disliked both wings of the state Democratic Party. Hundreds of volunteers just like Tom Luce had helped elevate Tower and wanted to do more to build their party. They gravitated to a young business leader who would guide them. The real work of building the party and the orchestration of Tower's victory was the accomplishment of one of the most skilled organizers Texas had yet seen—37-year-old Peter O'Donnell, now regarded as the true father of the Republican Party of Texas.

An up-and-coming business leader and securities investor, the ultraconservative O'Donnell was chair of the Dallas County Republican Party, where he was building a reliable bloc of voters for the GOP. He had already managed to leverage the anti-Communist hysteria that had gripped Dallas in the 1950s to elect the city's first Republican to the U.S. Congress: the right-wing ideologue Bruce Alger. But after the hateful events leading up to the Kennedy assassination, Dallas business leaders soured on the extremism of Alger and supported Democratic former mayor Earl Cabell, who defeated Alger in the 1964 general election. O'Donnell was savvy enough to understand that the Republicans needed to reach out beyond the extreme right to avoid scaring off Dallas's business leaders.

Even with all of Tom Luce's enthusiasm for the fledgling Republican movement, it took more than O'Donnell's efforts or the Dallas business establishment to provide an opportunity for Luce to be successful. It took Ross Perot, already one of the state's wealthiest entrepreneurs. Because of Perot and a few other visionary executives like him who had nothing to do with oil or cattle or the old Democratic Party battles, or even the Texas Regular segregationists, everything began to change in Texas.

FOUR

Blame It on Perot– and on Liberals, Too

WHEN YOU LOOK AT TOM LUCE'S SUCCESS IN law, business, and public service, and his 50 years as an influential Republican activist, it all goes back to flinty Ross Perot.

Nationally, Perot, the 1992 independent presidential candidate, has the reputation of "spoiler" in the race when Bill Clinton defeated George Herbert Walker Bush.[1] Perot has a much more important, but unrecognized, legacy as a visionary who helped turned Texas into a suburban bastion of Republican voters that would undermine a century of single-party state control by Democrats.

Tom Luce had just started his own law firm in Dallas when Perot handed him the legal business of his growing firm, Electronic Data Services (EDS). Perot founded EDS in 1962 and was quickly building the largest computer data management service company in the world. In Texas, however, it was Perot's unique vision for an EDS-style campus 20 miles north of Dallas that would spur suburban growth all over north Texas, make Tom Luce a fortune, and ultimately begin to inflate the big red bubble that covers Texas today.

Luce recalls riding horses with Perot across acres and acres of vacant prairie just north of Dallas in the late 1960s. "I couldn't see anything but scrub grass and a wide horizon," Luce said. But Perot saw the future. He had a vision for a vast technology campus that would house the nation's largest corporations that were riding the technology wave that was changing American business. Because he had been amalgamating land purchases for several years, Perot owned almost 2,500 acres in the area.

Perot believed that Texas needed to shift from an economy based largely on oil and gas production to a more diverse model based on knowledge and technical skills. He wanted to show how it could be done. He could see a cluster of cutting-edge technology companies rising from the flat prairie, with a modern EDS headquarters as its centerpiece. It would be surrounded by nice homes, good schools, lush parks, and other community amenities to attract workers from all across the nation. Perot's EDS was already pioneering a new kind of business that would grow because of brains, not brawn.

The technology growth spurt was already under way in Texas, spurred by a discovery that would revolutionize the fledgling computer industry. In 1958 Jack S. Kilby, a research engineer at Texas Instruments in Dallas, invented the microchip—a tiny crystal strip that could hold millions of bits of data in what is known as an integrated circuit. It would change business, popular culture, and the entire world economy and ultimately win Kilby a Nobel Prize. At the time, however, Kilby's laboratory was just a few miles down the road from Perot's original EDS headquarters.[2]

Perot had seen a residential housing boom reach into far North Dallas around Texas Instruments, but his plan for the EDS campus was much larger. He enlisted Tom Luce to do the grubby legal work and lobbying to make it happen.

As Perot's lawyer, Luce spent the next year negotiating with officials in Plano, a small town north of Dallas, to annex the land, build the roads, and create a vast utility infrastructure that could support Perot's campus. Plano had already experienced a growth spurt as middle-class white families began to flee Dallas in the 1960s to escape federal court–ordered desegregation of the schools. Now Plano was eager to expand its commercial tax base to support the quality schools its new residents were seeking. Plano's leaders were willing to think big enough to make Perot's vision a reality, but the complexity of the deal still required an enormous amount of time and negotiation to proceed. Finally, they succumbed to Luce's charm and persistence and unanimously approved everything Perot wanted.

When the gleaming EDS headquarters began to rise on the prairie, others grasped what Perot foresaw. Home builders and commercial real estate developers quickly followed, building shopping centers, apartment complexes, and small businesses, aided and abetted by a new North Texas Toll Authority, which in 1966 began its northward highway expansion toward Perot's EDS campus. Within a few years national corporations like Frito-Lay, J. C. Penney, Ericsson, Snapple-Dr. Pepper and others saw the synergy Perot envisioned and began relocating their headquarters adjacent to the EDS campus.

Perot's EDS venture attracted well-educated people from all over the country, including my own son-in-law, who left Boston immediately after college to come to Texas to work for EDS. With a declining economy in Rust Belt states brought on by automation, the demise of the steel and iron industries, the movement of manufacturing jobs to Asia, and the multilayered impact of globalization, cities like Detroit, Cleveland, Pittsburgh, and Buffalo lost more than 45 percent of their population between 1970 and 2006.[3] Displaced workers, especially middle managers and professionals, moved to the Sun Belt, where there were jobs, new housing, and "good"—mostly white—suburban schools. While Michigan, Ohio, and Pennsylvania were losing population, Texas was gaining. From 1970 to 1990, Texas grew from a little over 11 million residents to 17 million. Almost 60 percent of the growth of Texas in the 1970s was because of the influx of people from other states.

This movement from around the country to the mushrooming suburbs around Dallas, Houston, Austin, and San Antonio surpassed the first great migration to Texas in the aftermath of the Civil War, which drew white farmers from the Deep South who were broke and wanted new beginnings. They scribbled "GTT"—Gone to Texas—on their barns and homes when they left. With the decline of traditional industries in the Rust Belt, its professionals and high-wage workers were swept up in a second wave of GTT migration. Many of these families had a history of voting Republican and had no interest in the squabbles of Texas Democrats.

Between 1960 and 1980 the population of Collin County, home to Plano and EDS, grew from just under 41,700 to almost 145,000.[4] The opening of the Dallas–Fort Worth International

Airport in 1973 accelerated the pace of change in the area and provided corporate executives access to national and world markets. By 1980 the Dallas area had 650 companies whose net worth exceeded $1 million, the fourth most of any city in the United States.[5] Today, almost 900,000 people live in Collin County, and North Texas has become a suburban utopia—no longer rural, or poor, or isolated.[6]

All of this coincided with the work of Peter O'Donnell, who was building the organizational structure of the Texas Republican Party.

"O'Donnell just started canvassing his own neighborhood in North Dallas," Luce told me. The GOP activist would identify people who might vote Republican, put their names on a list, and then get volunteers to enter the information into an old IBM punch-card computer. "I remember going to some of those businesses that would let us use their computers after hours, and we started building files of potential Republican voters," Luce continued.

These early efforts in Dallas were the real beginning of the Republican Party in Texas, Luce believes. The first wave of suburban Dallas Republicans created the canvassing model, which later Republicans perfected. They had computerized neighborhood walk lists sorted by the voting history and interests of thousands of voters. Activists from Houston and other large Texas cities started coming to Dallas to learn from O'Donnell. Democrats at this stage were still using three-by-five note cards, if and when they had them, and looking up phone numbers on voter registration lists—aided by adolescents, like my younger sister and me, whose Democratic parents volunteered our help.

While O'Donnell was laying the groundwork for a truly sophisticated voter contact project, something else was happening nationally that allowed Texas Republicans to build a talented bench of officeholders who would change state and national politics in ways that still affect us today.

Voting Rights Act for All

In the 1960s, a series of federal court orders that altered voting districts in Texas broadened the playing field for both Democrats and Republicans—so much so that the Democrats barely noticed the unforeseen consequences. When minorities and liberal Democrats began winning legislative and congressional races, so did Republicans.

Inspired by the Civil Rights Act of 1964, Texas labor and civil rights lawyers began challenging the structure of large, countywide election districts that had blatantly diminished the vote and power of minority voters since the turn of the century. The most prominent among them was a young lawyer named David Richards.

"For me, civil rights was the incandescent issue of the day, and I desperately wanted to be part of the action," Richards remembered.[7] The Waco native attended Baylor University with his high-school sweetheart, Ann Willis. David and Ann Richards began their married life while still college students. After law school at the University of Texas at Austin, David joined one of the nation's premier labor-law firms, Mullinax & Wells in Dallas. While Ann was having babies and hosting dinner parties, David was representing low-wage workers in the San Antonio garment and meatpacking industries; the United Auto Workers on the assembly line at the huge General Motors plant outside Fort Worth; and the International Brotherhood of Teamsters union, which had a surprisingly strong presence in Texas.

More than labor law, however, it was civil rights and the unequal distribution of power in Texas that captured the imagination of David Richards. He knew that an unfettered right to vote—and the knowledge that one's vote would count equally—was the key to changing everything. From the mid-1960s to the mid-1970s, Richards and other lawyers from the Ralph Yarborough wing of the Democratic Party filed dozens of federal lawsuits challenging election districts so dominated by a majority of white voters that minority candidates had no chance of winning or even influencing the outcome for any progressive candidate. With a new mood in the country and an activist federal judiciary, the first barrier to minority voting to go was the poll tax, which a federal court ruled unconstitutional in 1966. Next came the composition of election districts throughout the state.

The 1960 census showed that one-fourth of Texas residents lived in just two counties—Dallas and Harris, where Houston is located. Yet the Texas Constitution limited these counties to only one member each in the Texas state senate, tilting political power to rural areas of the state. Since most of the state's minority voters lived in these urban areas, they were even more adversely affected because they had no representation in the Texas legislature in proportion to their numbers in the population. Because of the legal challenges brought by Richards and others, federal courts ruled that state senate districts had to be based on population rather than arbitrary county boundaries. The immediate effect of the rulings required the state to draw new districts to give urban areas like Dallas, Houston, and San Antonio more representation in the legislature. Houston picked up four senate seats, Dallas got three, and San Antonio now had two. Even more significant for minorities was the fact that the courts required that senators be elected from individual districts, based on "one person, one vote," thus giving them a greater opportunity to win or influence the outcome of these single-member districts.

Subsequent court orders required that single member individual districts replacing larger multi-member districts also be drawn for seats in the Texas House of Representatives. The court rulings and the newly drawn districts that went into effect for the 1966 elections created a sea change in Texas politics.[8]

One of the first beneficiaries of the new individual districts was the charismatic Barbara Jordan, of Houston, who became the first African American elected to the all-white Texas senate since Reconstruction, dramatic proof that the court decisions had changed the composition of the lily-white legislature practically overnight. In that same election two African Americans were elected to the state house: Joe Lockridge won a seat in Dallas, and Curtis Graves picked up a seat in Houston. Mexican Americans won significant victories as well: Lauro Cruz also picked up a legislative seat in Houston, and Joe Bernal won a state senate seat in San Antonio. With the influence of minority voters in numerous other individual districts, liberal white Democrats were also elected in Dallas, El Paso, and Houston. The adventurous *bon vivant* Charlie Wilson, immortalized in book and film, won a senate seat in East Texas with the help of a heavy black vote. But Republicans, too, gained from the more cohesive election districts, particularly in the more affluent neighborhoods of Houston and Dallas. Little noticed at the time by euphoric liberal Democrats was the Houston election of Hank Grover, the first Republican state senator since Reconstruction.

The GOP made an even more momentous leap into the future in 1966. After failing in his bid to unseat liberal U.S. senator Ralph Yarborough in 1964, George Herbert Walker Bush was elected to the U.S. Congress from Houston, a victory that created a chain of events that would impact Texas and national politics for decades.

In the next two election cycles Republicans, as well as minorities and liberal Democrats, would benefit from the individual election districts. By 1967, Dallas had a Republican in the state senate and another in the state house. By 1972, Republicans had elected 17 representatives to the state house, including Kay Bailey Hutchison, from Houston. That year three Republicans were also elected to the Texas senate.

With more Republicans seeking local office, the GOP primaries became more interesting, with real competition for races in the new, more cohesive voting districts. And with the movement of more voters into those GOP primaries, the longtime hold of conservative Democrats on all levels of power began to show a few cracks, particularly after Lyndon Johnson decided not to run for re-election in 1968. Many of his old financial backers within the major oil companies that had made Houston the center of the world's energy industry, could not abide the thought of liberal Democratic candidate Hubert Humphrey becoming president. The industry overwhelmingly supported Richard Nixon, and the 1968 presidential election was the end of oil money flowing to Democratic candidates in Texas, with the possible exception of Lloyd M. Bentsen, who defeated the old liberal warhorse Ralph Yarborough in a

U.S. Senate bid in 1970. The extent to which Texas conservatives would go to keep a Democrat out of the White House was evident in 1972, when more than $6.5 million in secret cash contributions from the Texas oil and gas industry was funneled into Nixon's re-election campaign in the months before federal campaign finance reporting laws went into effect. The fact that the money was secretly flown to Washington from Houston in a Pennzoil Oil Company plane was indicative of the shift of money and power away from Texas Democrats.[9]

Texas's Democratic Party was also changing during this period, becoming more progressive in tone and shedding many of its conservative leaders. The liberal wing of the party was helped along by a massive stock fraud and bribery scandal centered in the Sharpstown Bank in Houston. The 1971 scandal ended the careers of a half-dozen high-level conservative Democrats and sent a few of them to jail.[10] But it was a United Farm Workers strike, organized by Cesar Chavez in the Rio Grande Valley in the late 1960s, that energized Mexican Americans and gave the liberal wing of the party hope that its time was coming. The Texas AFL-CIO, at its peak membership of about 400,000, helped farm workers mount a statewide march to the capital that provided enough support for legislators to allow them to enact a $1.25 state minimum wage for farm workers and others not covered by federal minimum wage legislation, a solid departure from the Texas Way. Organized labor and liberal trial lawyers were also able to get a few progressives onto the Texas Supreme Court, which skewed its decisions in favor of ordinary individuals rather than the state's major businesses and industries, as had been its long-standing tradition.

The fledgling second-wave women's movement in Texas also brought new energy and candidates to the Texas political arena. At various times during the ten-year period between 1977 and 1987, every major Texas city—including Austin, Dallas, Houston, Fort Worth, and San Antonio—was headed by a female mayor.

Liberals Hit the Jackpot

Few events seemed to herald a new era in Texas politics more than the 1976 election of fun-loving, liberal Ann Richards as the county commissioner who represented the western part of Travis County, home to the beautiful capital city of Austin.

In the 1970s, Austin surged with the vitality of students who came from all over the world to attend the University of Texas. The intellectual center of the state, the city had a thriving honky-tonk bar culture that captivated local liberals and even conservative members of the Texas legislature, who packed the local watering holes when they came to town. Austin was always more progressive than the rest of the state, but in 1971 Austin's Democratic base grew overnight after the 26th Amendment to the U.S. Constitution granted 18-year-olds the right to vote. In one election cycle, more than 25,000 new student voters pumped up Austin's liberal elite. Equally important, the city was about to become a major center for technology and innovation. A group of visionary business leaders had created several technology incubators, luring national and international companies to Austin to take advantage of the city's skilled workforce.

Largely centered in Austin's growing progressive scene, the core group of friends who helped Richards get elected to local office in 1976 had gotten to know one another by participating in the founding of the Texas Women's Political Caucus. In the early 1970s, they established a Women's Center to amalgamate social services for women. They also created a nonprofit foundation to promote women's history; established the state's first rape crisis center; and began one of the nation's first intensive leadership development programs for women. By 1973, they had helped win passage of a state version of the Equal Rights Amendment and had gotten the state legislature to ratify the national ERA, which later failed to be approved by enough states to become part of the U.S. Constitution.[11]

During this progressive interlude, Ann Richards and I became friends and colleagues. After years of volunteering for political campaigns, Richards took on a more professional role as campaign manager for 27-year-old Sarah Weddington's first race for the Texas legislature in 1972. Weddington, a lawyer, was basking in the national spotlight after her stunning U.S. Supreme Court victory arguing *Roe v. Wade*, the challenge that made abortion legal in every state in the nation.

Richards and I had gotten to know each other through our husbands. David Richards was general counsel for the Texas AFL-CIO, and my husband, John Rogers, was its legislative and political director. I was working for Texas Land Commissioner Bob Armstrong, who brought an environmentalist's sensibility to the management of Texas's 22 million acres of state-owned land. Armstrong gave me free rein over all aspects of agency management— from handling press operations to writing grievance procedures and developing the agency's budget. Because I was learning about the internal workings of state government, Ann began calling me every few weeks, asking for help with one task or another for Sarah Weddington's campaign. The conversations always began with Ann sweetly pleading in that distinctive Texas twang, "MB, I need your help." She usually wanted me to write up a mail piece or brochure to persuade Austin's state employees, numbering about 12,000 at the time, to vote for Weddington. Ann had already become such a sparkling presence on the Austin political and party scene that I never had the nerve to turn her down. I spent many evenings at home banging out mail pieces for the Weddington campaign. When Weddington won, Ann decided that she too would run for office, and those phone calls kept coming. I was deeply involved in her race for county commissioner, again taking multiple volunteer assignments, including producing her television commercials— quite a learning experience for me. By the time Ann took office in early 1977, we had decided that we made a pretty good working team. If Ann could think something up, I would try to figure out a way to do it.

The 1970s were heady days for liberals, women, and Ann Richards. We were riding high on a nascent feminist movement under way in Texas. To some degree, conservative Republican women also caught the bug and were determined to prove their influence within their own party. Upscale women had been a reliable source of Republican volunteers since John Tower's Senate campaign in 1961; after his election, they established a network of Republican women's clubs across the state. By the mid-1970s, more than 6,000 women belonged to those clubs, largely organized by Rita Bass Clements, the Republican National Committee member from Texas.[12] And it would be her husband, Bill Clements, who would bring the Republican Party to full maturity in Texas.

FIVE

Permanent Breakthrough

ALTHOUGH BILL CLEMENTS WAS A REPUBLI-
can stalwart in Texas, no one expected or particularly wanted him
to run for governor in the GOP primary in 1978. Few thought he
could win if he did.

A Dallas native, Clements started out as a roughneck oil driller
while Texas was still in the heyday of its oil boom. He was smart
and tough, with a gruffness that was de rigueur among those willing to risk their lives and money to find oil. He began to specialize
in the dangerous process of ocean drilling. In Texas, which claimed
territory up to ten miles into the Gulf of Mexico, there was plenty
of offshore oil to be had. In 1947, he founded the company that
would come to be known as SEDCO, the world's largest offshore
driller and pioneer of many of the innovations that made deep-
water drilling possible. By the early 1960s he had developed a
business partnership with George H. W. Bush, whose affiliations

with Zapata Petroleum and Pennzoil had made him a key player in the Texas energy establishment.

Although Clements had always considered himself to be an independent, he recoiled at the liberal direction of the Texas and national Democratic Parties. As his wealth grew, he began to lend his financial support to Republican candidates. He had encouraged George H. W. Bush to make what would be a losing run against Ralph Yarborough for Senate in 1964 and supported Bush's ultimately successful race for Congress in 1966. Clements once boasted that he had put at least a half million dollars into Bush's campaigns, because "That's what politics is all about, isn't it!"[1] By 1968, Clements had become a prodigious fund-raiser for Richard Nixon. As a reward, Nixon made him deputy secretary of defense, under Donald Rumsfeld, and Clements stayed on at Gerald Ford's request after he assumed the presidency when Nixon resigned. After the election of Democrat Jimmy Carter in 1976, Clements returned to Texas but was not quite ready to retire. He thought he could do a better job as governor than any of the Democrats who had held the job during his lifetime. He and his second wife, Rita Bass Clements, knew a thing or two about Texas politics—and particularly about the power of money, which they had in abundance.

In November 1977, when Clements announced that he would run for governor, his brash personality and self-confidence were on full display as he dressed down a skeptical Texas press gaggle that questioned his reasons for running. *Who was this gruff old guy who thought he could become the first Republican governor in Texas in more than 100 years?* "If you people have some idea that I'm doing this for experience, you're dreaming," he told the reporters. "I need to make this race just like I need a hole in the head. I'm in this thing to win, and if I didn't think I could win, I wouldn't be in it. Any other questions?"[2]

Because of his experience in the oil fields, Clements believed that he could connect with ordinary Texas voters in a visceral way. Although he was part of the wealthy Dallas country club establishment, Clements maintained the common touch of a roughneck. Despite his wife's best efforts, he never seemed to care if his ever-present plaid sports jackets were in fashion or not.

In the 1978 primary, he swiftly dispatched the Republican Party's state chair, Ray Hutchison, a prominent Dallas bond lawyer who had been instrumental in building the party statewide. Even then, no one thought that Clements had a chance to win. But off-year elections have a funny way of tripping up surefire bets.

Once again, feuding Texas Democrats handed Republicans a gift. In a stunning upset orchestrated by my late husband, John Rogers, Attorney General John Hill defeated the incumbent governor, Dolph Briscoe, in the Democratic primary.

John and I had moved to Austin in the early 1970s when he had the opportunity to head public relations and legislative affairs for the Texas AFL-CIO. After a while, he struck out on his own to run campaigns, including Hill's 1972 campaign for attorney general. Coming out of the liberal wing of the Democratic Party, John considered Briscoe and his team to be just like those old conservatives who had always run state government—simply less vigorous. Hill, on the other hand, had the intellectual capacity and vitality to become an outstanding governor with a bias for action that could improve the state.

John Hill was a brilliant Houston trial attorney so renowned for his lisping oratory that young lawyers would flock to the courtroom just to hear his arguments. Hill was so impressive that conservative governor John Connally appointed Hill secretary of state in 1966, giving him his first taste of political life in Austin. He liked it so much that he ran for governor in 1968 but lost in a crowded field. By 1972, he was ready to venture out again, this time running for attorney general and winning. However, contrary to expectations of the conservative Democratic leaders who had supported him, Hill became an activist, reform-minded attorney general. He set up a consumer protection division within his office, as well as a fledgling environmental protection operation. Most importantly, he built up a team of public interest lawyers who had been influenced by Ralph Nader and would shape Texas policies and regulatory agencies for the next two decades.

Conservative Democrats were first of all amazed that John Hill would challenge so benign a figure as Briscoe, and then they were *really* stunned that Hill actually defeated him. Briscoe was a veritable symbol of the old Texas Way: a wealthy cattle rancher, a no-new-taxes fiscal conservative, and a "let's not shake things up too much" kind of governor who was content to preserve the status quo.

After knocking off Briscoe, Hill looked unbeatable in the general election. He was self-confident and savvy in public relations and smooth as silk in his demeanor. Clements, in contrast, was rough around the edges, argumentative, and didn't give a hoot what Texas news reporters thought of him.

Aces in the Hole

Clements figured he had a couple of aces in the hole when he began the race—the 400,000-plus conservative Democrats who had crossed over to vote for Ronald Reagan against Gerald Ford in the 1976 Republican primary, and those who voted for Briscoe over Hill. The wild card in the game was Jimmy Carter's cratering popularity. Rita and Bill Clements and Republican Party state chair Peter O'Donnell knew how to go after these discontented voters.

Although Clements tried and failed to get the embittered Democratic governor Briscoe to endorse him publicly, Briscoe had no objections when his adult children came out for Clements, or even when his wife said she thought that Clements would be a better governor than Hill.[3] But Reagan was Clements's big prize, and several of the ex-California governor's former campaign staffers came to Texas to help the Clements effort. When Reagan made a swing through Texas to appear with Clements, the duo drew huge, enthusiastic crowds. Clements had been trailing badly in most early public opinion polls, but Reagan's visit gave him a boost.

Clements began painting John Hill with the stain of Jimmy Carter's increasingly dismal presidency. When Carter endorsed Hill, Clements had all he needed to complete the liberal portrait of John Hill. Clements roused crossover Democrats with issues like school busing, school prayer, gun control, anti-Communism, and abortion restrictions. While the traditional "Red Scare" had played well in Texas elections since World War II, this was the first time that social and cultural issues had led the way in a statewide election. A right-to-life movement had emerged in Texas after the U.S. Supreme Court's decision on *Roe v. Wade,* and by 1976, anti-abortion activists were becoming an important element in the Republican Party's base.

Republican rhetoric was fierce, frightening, and constant, but Hill was loath to hit hard in return. He was already warming to the role of statesman and brushed off the impact of the attacks. He refused to let his staff respond in kind. But by holding back and letting many of the attacks go unanswered, Hill unwittingly allowed the Clements campaign to capitalize on fear among conservatives that their old, comfortable Democratic Party had become a hotbed of liberals and libertines. In 1978, twice as many Texans identified themselves as Democrats than as Republicans, but twice as many also identified themselves as conservative rather than liberal.[4] Those conservative Democrats would be targeted mercilessly.

Bill and Rita Clements made sure that one or the other would visit each of Texas's 254 counties, a rare feat that few candidates—Democrat or Republican—managed to achieve. Clements even met with local Democratic officials to reassure them that he was on their side. His campaign set up active organizations in 130 rural counties, most headed by conservative Democrats.

While the Clementses were traveling all over Texas, an overconfident John Hill took the summer off. He was already planning his transition into the governor's office. By the time he reentered the hustings after Labor Day, the tide was beginning to turn against him—he just refused to acknowledge it. As late as two weeks before the November election Hill bragged to reporters that a *Texas Monthly* poll showed he was leading Clements by 11 points. But internal polls in both campaigns actually showed that the race was neck and neck.[5] Campaign manager Rogers and his deputy, Jack Martin, knew the race was too close to call and that the campaign would have to double up on television spots and its GOTV efforts. Martin remembers that Hill was so sure that he could count on the votes of Democratic traditionalists that he refused to let his staff spend the money to counter Clements's attacks or put in a last-ditch effort to pump a large Democratic turnout.[6] As it turned out, that was a fatal mistake.

The final week of the campaign was one of misery in our home. John knew that Hill was about to lose, but because his hands were tied, he couldn't stop it. Post-election polls showed that about one-third of voters made up their minds during the last week of the campaign.[7] Those undecided votes fell to Clements rather than to Hill. The margin was so close that the lead changed several times during the overnight vote count, but Clements managed to pull out a victory with a little over 16,000 votes out of 2.2 million cast.

Clements's election was a victory for the old Texas Way—just with a different label. William Broyles, writing in *Texas Monthly*, recognized that Clements was a "walking Texas myth, just as, in his own way, Dolph Briscoe was. Briscoe was the archetypal rancher; Clements is the roughneck. Each monopolized one of the state's two most potent symbols: cattle and oil."[8] Despite the progressive trends in the Texas legislature during the 1970s, the 1978 election proved that cattle and oil were still in control.

The Clements victory was a spur for conservative Democrats to switch their party allegiance to the Republicans. Future U.S. senator Phil Gramm, then a Democratic member of Congress from College Station, quit the Democrats in 1983 and was successfully reelected as a Republican. A number of other Democrats soon followed suit, including Congressman Kent Hance of Lubbock.

When Clements took office in early 1979, Texas had four Republicans and 20 Democrats in the U.S. House of Representatives. At home, his party counted four Republicans among the 31 senators and 22 Republicans in the state house. But that was not quite enough to help Clements enact his own policies. Flush with his victory and full of ideas about how to cut taxes and trim bureau-cracy, Clements soon faced the reality that it was the Democratic-controlled legislature that held power over the governor, not the other way around. With both a Democratic lieutenant governor and Speaker of the House on their side, the majority of Democrats did not jump when the brash Clements expected them to. Clements had a fairly rough first legislative session, failing to secure his bare-bones budget or to shape policy in the ways he envisioned. After the legislature overrode his veto of an uncontested "local" bill—the kind that the legislature frequently passed as a favor to satisfy some legislator's local constituent—Clements responded by calling members "a bunch of idiots."[9]

Catalyst for Change

If the Democrats in the legislature didn't care much for the brash new governor, he proved to be an inspiration to a number of ambi-tious young Republicans. They started coming together regularly in a group they dubbed "Camp Wannameetagop."[10] The brain-child of lawyer and journalist Doug Harlan and Cyndi Taylor Krier, who went on to be a state senator from San Antonio, the informal group was dedicated to building a network of campaign activists. With most in their 30s and 40s, the initial members ulti-mately became the Republican establishment in Texas. Kay Bailey Hutchison and John Cornyn would become U.S. senators, and oth-ers would become members of Congress, serve as federal judges, and build powerful organizations in their local areas. In the 1970s and '80s, they met periodically for drinks, gossip, and strategy, and give personal encouragement to one another as they embarked on their own political careers. They were tremendously successful in extending their network of supporters and funders.

By 1980, Governor Clements had a new cause. He was determined to help Ronald Reagan throw Jimmy Carter out of office. Clements took personal affront at Carter's Crude Oil Windfall Profit Tax Act, signed during the height of the 1970s global energy crisis. He launched a major effort that would guarantee Republican dominance in Texas for the next 25 years.

Clements served as chair of the Reagan-Bush campaign in Texas and raised more than $2.5 million to invest in a massive Republican GOTV push. He also headed a Reagan-Bush Texas Victory Committee, which organized phone banks in all 254 Texas counties. His group also sent out half a million pieces of mail to undecided voters, 84,000 letters to conservatives, and more than 800,000 pieces of mail to rural voters.[11] The Republicans didn't stop there. Because their goal was to get 25 percent of the Hispanic vote, they mailed more than 250,000 letters to voters with Hispanic surnames. Clements used his influence to line up prestige endorsements for Reagan from some of Texas's greatest sports heroes: Roger Staubach, Nolan Ryan, and the much-revered Dallas Cowboys coach Tom Landry. It was the most massive Republican effort in Texas history, and it worked. Reagan carried Texas by an impressive 13 percent margin. It was this pivotal election that gave Karl Rove his first taste of victory in Texas politics.

Rove had moved to Texas in 1977 after dabbling with the College Republicans at several schools and marrying a Texas girl who wanted to go home. He worked briefly for George H. W. Bush, and through Bush had gotten to know Bill Clements. After Clements took office in 1979, he hired Rove for various political tasks and was impressed enough with his work to make him executive director of the Reagan-Bush Texas Victory Committee. During the campaign, Rove had the opportunity to learn from the master of Texas Republican politics—Peter O'Donnell. It was O'Donnell who taught Rove about campaign budgeting, strategy, and how to build grassroots organizations.[12] Under O'Donnell's tutelage Rove mastered the art of direct-mail fund-raising, sending out over a million pieces of direct mail for the Reagan-Bush ticket in Texas. After the election, with O'Donnell's financial backing, Rove set up a direct-mail business in Austin and became a general consultant to several Republican candidates.

In the 1980 presidential election, the Republican success in mobilizing conservative voters—ranging from working-class populists to evangelical Christians to suburban-dwelling traditionalists to aspiring business leaders and fraternity and sorority alumni—initiated the slow death march of the Democratic Party in Texas.[13] No Democratic presidential candidate has carried Texas since then.

Wayne Thorburn, executive director of the state Republican Party when Clements became governor, believes the 1980 presidential election was the pivotal event that began to change Texas: "Ronald Reagan had made it more than acceptable to be a Republican for Texas conservatives, he had made it expected. In so doing, he had broken one of the critical bases of the Texas Democratic Party—its 'yellow-dog' conservatives, whose loyalty to the party had been built on tradition and conformity. For the next two decades, this base would continue to turn out for local Democratic candidates in much of rural Texas, but the base was eroding away."[14]

The proof is in the numbers.

When Clements took office in 1979, Republicans held 87 county offices. By 1996 that number had jumped to 938, and by 2012, party members held more than 2,000 local offices.[15]

Although he was largely responsible for the organizational effort that allowed the Reagan victory, Clements couldn't hold on to his own office in 1982. The economy was sagging because of a drop in the price of oil, and his drilling company, SEDCO, was involved in the largest offshore well blowout in history at the time, the Ixtoc I spill, which caused extensive environmental damage. Clements was somewhat tainted by the disaster. In his reelection campaign, he faced another Democratic attorney general, Mark White, who had been elected during the same race that brought Clements to power. But White was much more conservative than his predecessor, John Hill, and he managed to unify the party rather than divide it. By the end of Clements's term, liberal and conservative Democrats alike had had their fill of the governor's gruff style and came together to support White.

The Gang of Four

The 1982 general election in Texas was as significant for liberal Democrats as the 1980 election had been for conservative Republicans. Along with Mark White's defeat of Clements, voters swept into office the most liberal slate of statewide officials Texas had ever seen. Lloyd Bentsen, who was seeking his third term in the U.S. Senate after defeating Ralph Yarborough in 1970, provided the leadership and organizational structure that made the victories possible.

Bentsen's top aide and campaign manager, Jack Martin, had been involved in John Hill's losing race for governor four years earlier, and based on his experience in that campaign, Martin knew that the popular senator could not automatically count on reelection against his Republican challenger, the well-financed U.S. congressman James Collins of Dallas.

"Bentsen was determined that the Republicans would not do to him what they had done to John Hill in 1978," Martin remembers. The senator decided to put his money and staff into a massive GOTV-based campaign, conceived and implemented by Martin. His 1982 coordinated GOTV campaign for all the statewide candidates became the model later used in Ann Richards's 1990 winning race for governor. The success of these efforts made Martin the go-to guy in Democratic Party circles.[16] But later, his involvement in his expanding private businesses ventures kept him out of the Texas political fray—and out of the spotlight.

What struck political reporters most about the 1982 Democratic victories, however, was the election of four flaming liberals to the remaining top offices in the state. They were soon dubbed the "Gang of Four." Far from being mere tag-alongs on Bentsen's coattails, each had donated funds and hands to the coordinated campaign and was a serious contender in his or her own right.

The new liberal office holders included Ann Richards, who moved up from her county post to be the new state treasurer. She became the first woman elected to a statewide office in 50 years, thanks to a huge core of volunteers eager to see a woman in office. Jim Mattox, a former congressman from Dallas who was elected attorney general, had strong support from organized labor. Populist former editor of the famed *Texas Observer*, Jim Hightower, became the state's agriculture commissioner. And the new land commissioner, Garry Mauro, had toiled in the trenches for Ralph Yarborough and had become best friends with Hillary Rodham and Bill Clinton when they campaigned together in Texas for George McGovern in 1972.

These were not insignificant victories for the liberal wing of the Democratic Party. Richards handled the state's money, Mattox took care of the state's legal business, Hightower looked out for Texas farmers, and Mauro became steward of 22 million acres of state-owned land and the oil and gas royalties that flowed from them. They were the new face of power in Texas.

Yet the smashing victory for the liberals obscured a swelling Republican tide building across the state. There were troubling signs for Democrats, even in 1982.

Matthew Dowd, who worked for Jack Martin, was among the first to see the change. "After each election, I always wrote a memo analyzing the outcome," Dowd said. When he looked at the 1982 data, he saw something stunning. Even though Bentsen had won with 59 percent of the vote, he had lost the white vote. Dowd's memo to Martin was stark in its warning about the loss of white voters, and it predicted bad days ahead for the Democrats. "Watch out! Here it comes," he wrote.[17]

Democratic pollster Richard Murray was also seeing some of the same shifts in how voters described themselves in the early 1980s. "If you were a conservative, you no longer identified yourself as a Democrat," he said. After Bill Clements had been in office, Murray began to see more people identify themselves as Independents. "But within an election cycle or two, I began to see more self-identified Republicans. They might still vote in a Democratic primary election, where most of the action was, but come November they were fully in the Republican column. It only took a few years before they made the formal switch to Republican."[18]

It was amid this unsettling, swelling red tide that liberal Democrats finally got their chance to lead Texas.

SIX

The Illusion of Victory

IN 1983, ANN RICHARDS AND I WENT TO A meeting of the National Association of State Treasurers in Jackson Hole, Wyoming. Ann was in her first year as state treasurer of Texas and I was the deputy treasurer. We were the two highest-ranking women in Texas government.

One afternoon, as we were waiting to take a guided raft ride on the Snake River, we were both overcome with the beauty of Grand Teton National Park and the coolness of the fresh mountain air. (It was summer, and we Texans get a little giddy when we find a bit of relief from our intense heat, especially when we get to wear jackets to ward off a chill.) Ann, always full of great quips and impeccable timing, suggested that we ought to get our core group of women friends to move to cool Wyoming and take over its politics. After all, it was the least populous state in the union—not much bigger than Austin, where we lived—and Wyoming had elected the nation's first woman governor back in 1924. It might not be that hard to do it again. For the next few minutes we joked and played out our fantasy about which of our friends would hold top offices: Ann, of course, would be the governor.

Seven years later, it was not little old Wyoming that we took over. We took over the big, bad State of Texas. Or so we thought. Ann Richards was governor. I was her chief of staff. We brought into government some of the smartest people in Texas who had a sense of the common good and a commitment to ethical practices. We took over the state's regulatory agencies, promoted economic development, and changed the look of state government through the governor's power to appoint members of state boards and commissions. Never before in Texas history had so many women, African Americans, Hispanics, liberals, consumer advocates, gays, labor leaders, environmentalists, and ordinary people been appointed to so many seats in the halls of power.

Of course, we didn't do all of this by ourselves. Ann Richards's election in 1990 was the result of a unique constellation of timing, events, and people, most notably Jack Martin, who would go on to head Hill + Knowlton Strategies, the global public relations juggernaut. It was he who persuaded me to take over the campaign for the general election and who became a confidant and guiding star for Ann Richards. Working with us was Matthew Dowd, who at the time was considered the best "numbers guy" in Texas and who would later use his expertise to help George W. Bush become president of the United States. The late, great media guru Bob Squire created memorable television spots for Richards and instinctively knew how to hit hard at an opponent. We had a small press team, headed by former *Houston Post* reporter Glenn Smith, and an ace fund-raiser in Jennifer Treat. George Shipley put together a research team par excellence, and Suzanne

Coleman continued in her role as Ann's primary speechwriter. Jane Hickie and Cathy Bonner rounded out the staff and friends who understood the myriad complexities, myths, and realities of Texas.[1] Every one of Ann's four children played a major role in the campaign, as did her son-in-law Kirk Adams, who was field director.

What made it all work was that we had pulled together the warring factions of the badly fractured Democratic Party structure that had almost blown apart during a brutal three-way race for the nomination that had pitted former governor Mark White against Attorney General Jim Mattox and Richards, who was smack dab in the political center of the two. After the primary, Richards was able to create a new coalition that included organized labor, teachers, Hispanics, African Americans, Anglo liberals, trial lawyers, disability organizations, players in the small-but-growing gay rights movement, and the remnants of the old-style Johnson-Connally fiscal conservatives who had stayed loyal to their party. Critical to our success was an energetic and committed group of suburban women riding the crest of second-wave feminism. This included Richards's core group of women friends who had worked together on projects large and small over the years.

Women were particularly inspired by Ann Richards and wanted to see her in the governor's office. They were not alone. Texans had never seen such a good-old girl who was as dynamic, funny, smart, charming, or good-looking as Ann Richards. She could speak the language of ordinary country folks and even won over the beer-bellied guys who appreciated a feisty woman every now and then. She was Texan to the core and had the twang to prove it.

Of course, the victory was sweet. We were euphoric, proud, full of ourselves, and determined to build a New Texas. But the election was a fluke, an aberration, a last-minute flash in the pan—not gold but brass, soon to be tarnished by reality. The real question was how a divorced single mother, civil rights activist, pro-choice feminist, and recovering alcoholic could have ever been elected in the first place. With Ann Richards's election the natural order of traditional, conservative Texas politics seemed to have been upended.

The Republican tide in Texas was already surging, delayed (we now know) only by a hapless millionaire who happened to be Richards's Republican opponent. Oilman Clayton Williams, who spent a fortune to win the Republican primary, made one gaffe after another during the race against Richards. When telling a crude joke, he advised women who were raped to simply lie back and enjoy it. He refused to shake Ann's hand during a joint television appearance, a decidedly ungentlemanly thing to do in traditional Texas. After much goading on our part, he admitted that, despite his millions, he had managed to avoid paying income taxes for the past few years. Williams gave the Richards campaign the good luck so desperately needed to win. But to our credit, we actually had a strategy and plan to overcome the 27-point advantage Williams carried at the outset of the race.

We pounced quickly on every gaffe, misstatement, and error the Republican made. As time went on, we got pretty good at forcing the arrogant and undisciplined candidate to keep on making mistakes.

We savored his defeat, but what we didn't realize at the time was that the big red Republican bubble soon to engulf Texas was already beginning to fill with hot air. Although Ann Richards won the general election by about 100,000 votes, she didn't quite crack the 50 percent mark, drawing 49.4 percent of the vote.

Furthermore, Republicans managed to win three important statewide offices. For the first time they were capturing second-tier offices never held by Republicans before. Democrat-turned-Republican Rick Perry defeated firebrand Jim Hightower for agriculture commissioner; Kay Bailey Hutchison was elected to Richards's old office as state treasurer; and John Cornyn was elected to the Texas Supreme Court. Karl Rove had consulted for each of them.

Republicans were also capturing local offices, becoming county commissioners, sheriffs, and county clerks in charge of the state's voting mechanisms. We obviously didn't realize it at the time, but by 1990 the stage was being set for the next go-round.

Fast-forward to 1994: The Clinton presidency was in disarray. The off-year election gave Republicans control of the U.S. House of Representatives, embodied by Newt Gingrich and his Contract with America. Popular New York governor Mario Cuomo was defeated in a Democratic stronghold and, of course, Ann Richards lost in Texas. George W. Bush was the lucky guy who rode the prevailing wind into her office. Because of the national sweep in 1994, and the fact that Texas was already so clearly a Republican-leaning state, it is now apparent that any credible Republican candidate would have defeated Richards that year. It did not take the son of a president and his handler, Karl Rove, to make it happen. They were simply in the right place at the right time.

Those of us close to Richards who were so jubilant when she won in 1990 must admit that we were just plain lucky then, instead of the brilliant strategists we imagined ourselves to be. If the Republicans had put up a credible candidate instead of a clown, Ann Richards probably never would have become governor in the first place. The irony is that if the Democrats had put up any candidate other than Ann Richards, that candidate would certainly have lost—even to Clayton Williams. Only someone as salty, charismatic, and unique as Ann could have brought forth the tasteless, sexist, and stupid statements of such a politically inept neophyte as Williams.

Richards had built a centrist record as the treasurer who cleaned up the state's antiquated financial system. In the beginning, the public did not see her as some radical leftist, even though she never hid her background as a civil rights activist or pro-choice feminist. But after four years of relentless attacks against her, Texans began to consider that she might be *one of those* horrible Democrats like Bill Clinton, who threatened their values, their livelihood, their property, and, most importantly, their guns.

A New Texas Experiment

As I reflect on my time in the governor's office with Ann Richards, I realize that we tried to govern as if we had won a revolution. Heady with our victory, we set out to construct a New Texas. Before the old crowd that had always dominated state politics and power had a chance to realize what was happening, we managed to initiate—and inflict—some major changes in Texas public policy. We tackled it all—high insurance rates, air and water pollution, hazardous waste disposal, lack of transparency in state purchasing contracts, new ethics rules for officeholders, Texas's lax regulatory enforcement practices, the unequal distribution of state funds to rich and poor school districts, and on and on and on.

Texas had never seen such a rapid rush of progressive policies or diverse people in charge, and it didn't take long for the army of lobbyists for the state's most powerful economic interests to figure out what was going on. Grumblings about "those crazy staffers"—those uppity women and lefty men who worked with them in the governor's office—could soon be heard in Capitol corridors. Then it grew to a growl that leaked out to the press corps, always hungry for a bit of gossip or conflict. Finally, it reached a menacing roar that blasted out across the state, particularly after Ann Richards vetoed legislation that would have allowed Texans to carry concealed handguns. The Bush campaign picked it up as a great battle cry for the believers in the old Texas Way: Ann Richards was going to take away your guns, your property, and local control of your schools.

The real opposition to Richards, however, did not derive from whom she did or didn't appoint or what she did or didn't do about guns. Business leaders were sophisticated enough in the ways of the world to know that none of that really mattered. Who cared if Ann Richards flooded state agencies with blacks, Mexican Americans, gays, labor goons, hordes of women, or even purple Martians? What actually did matter was that these upstarts believed they could change Texas, and by God, they were in the process of trying to do so. So all the attempts to open the power of state government to ordinary folks—which made us all so proud—were saved up and later used as campaign fodder aimed at white voters who seemed to fear the complexities brought on by the massive cultural changes under way across the nation.

Our efforts to bring progressive policies and inclusive politics to Texas had brought about a violent reaction among those who had always held power—the insurance and chemical industries, the financial institutions, the real estate developers, the oil and gas producers, the trucking and construction firms, the utilities, and even the liquor distributors. By the end of Ann's first year in office, these interests had already coalesced around the barely concealed candidacy of George W. Bush, and it was widely known that he was being carefully groomed for a gubernatorial run by ambitious political consultant Karl Rove. But Bush was no innocent. And Rove was no genius.

Already well entrenched in the state's powerful oil and gas industry and in national Republican politics, thanks to his father's connections, Bush had long hobnobbed with Texas's big rich political players. It should have surprised no one that he emerged rather quickly as a disciplined contender, schooled in political niceties and careful to avoid the kinds of insensitive comments about women that had helped sink Clayton Williams. The public campaign took the high ground, focusing entirely on education improvements, crime reduction, and tort reform. But a well-funded stealth campaign was all about guns and gays.

In the November 1994 general election, genial good-time guy George W. Bush trounced tart-tongued Ann Richards and all of those who had put their hope into a New Texas. Bush won by an astounding million-vote margin in a 54–45 percent victory.

Well . . . what did we expect? We had challenged the most powerful economic interests in the state, and of course they were going to come after us with whatever they could piece together. Those who have privilege and influence rarely give it up willingly, especially to a bunch of liberals who turned out to be a much larger threat than anyone could have imagined.

I guess we were a little too much like the "children of light" that theologian Reinhold Niebuhr wrote about in the 1940s. Niebuhr's analysis of liberal politics revealed that do-gooders often underestimate how raw power can be used against them. As a result, they repeatedly set themselves up for disaster and defeat. He called naïve practitioners of liberalism "children of light." In contrast, "children of darkness" hold a rather cynical view of politics that recognizes no power or authority greater than their own. They are willing to use any means necessary to protect their interests. Niebuhr, a supreme realist, understood that there is always a conflict between self-interest and the general interest in a democratic society. Children of light are so sure that they are promoting the general interest that they are unaware of how self-righteous they often appear. Children of darkness understand how to use the power of the strong over the weak in ways the children of light rarely do. Niebuhr advised his liberal friends to study the forces against them, to learn to be as wily as their opponents, and then "beguile, deflect, harness, and restrain" them for the sake of the community.[2] It was all a riff, of course, on Jesus's instruction to his disciples to be wise as serpents and innocent as doves.[3]

We did not quite have the wisdom or wily temperament that Niebuhr advocated. I'm not sure it would have mattered much at the time, anyway. We never really held the power we thought we had claimed. A more disturbing thought is that perhaps we ended up helping Texas—with its enormous economic might and the individual personal fortunes that bankroll high-dollar independent expenditure campaigns that minimize the influence of ordinary voters—become the reddest wacko state in the union.

The essence of conservative politics in modern life has always been to reclaim what is lost, or is about to be lost, if power slips away. That's what happened in Texas in the 1990s. It has happened repeatedly since then.

Few Democrats saw the magnitude or long-term implications of Ann Richards's defeat. The conventional wisdom was that she lost because it was a bad year for Democrats, or that George W. Bush had the advantage of a famous name, or the voting base just did not show up in the numbers they expected. Some even perceived that the 1994 campaign was simply not as well-run as the effort had been in 1990, and that Richards herself didn't seem to want to win as badly as in the first race, either. There was more truth in those insights than any of us wanted to admit. In a strange sort of way, Richards actually seemed as much relieved as disappointed on election night. After her concession call, she quipped, "I think I've just added another ten years to my life because of what happened tonight."

Perils of Frustration and Fatigue

In 1994, Ann Richards was just plain worn out. Typical of many women of her generation, who came of age in the 1950s, she believed that she had to work twice as hard to appear half as smart as most of the men she dealt with. From her early days as governor to her last frantic days of campaigning, she carried around folders of policy briefs, staff memos, and constituent correspondence, and she plowed through every single item every single night. Those of us who were close to her saw the gray fatigue that settled over her like a transparent shroud. We had seen it a lot earlier, too—even before the campaign got under way. She was like the ballerina played by Moira Shearer in the classic 1948 movie *The Red Shoes*. Because the dancer wanted to be a star, she put on the magic red ballet slippers that wouldn't let her stop dancing until she collapsed.[4] Ann couldn't stop dancing—or working—and we worried about her health and well-being.

In 1993, when Bush's entry into the governor's race began to look like a sure thing, Jack Martin, Jane Hickie, and I scheduled a private lunch with Ann for one of those Texas-style "come to Jesus" conversations. We had become a troika of truth-tellers in Ann's life and were willing to risk her displeasure when we brought up topics she didn't want to touch. Hickie, a lawyer, was Ann's closest friend and advisor and had run her first campaign for county commissioner back in 1974. At the time Jane was serving as head of the Texas Office of State-Federal Relations in Washington, where her job was to bring home federal projects and funding. Martin, of course, had had a storied career in Texas politics as a legendary behind-the-scenes strategist before he launched a successful public relations business, troubleshooting for clients like AT&T, Southwest Airlines, and dozens of Fortune 100 companies. Yet Martin kept his ear to the political ground and knew that a hard-hitting Bush campaign against a vulnerable incumbent would be no picnic. We had all been with Ann through the dark days when she went through treatment for alcoholism, and each of us had played important personal and political roles in her life since then.

During our lunch, I remember Jack telling Ann that it would be okay if she decided not to run for reelection. She could leave office at the peak of her popularity, have a bright future on the national scene, and be able to do anything else she wanted. Most importantly, she could walk away from the stresses of daily Republican attacks and move on to a calmer, healthier life. Jane and I fully concurred. We laid out a case for stepping aside, but Ann would have none of it.

"Y'all don't understand," she shot back. "I have to run. Too many people—too many women—depend on me. If I give up now, I'd let them all down."[5]

Ann Richards certainly didn't give up in 1994. She was a born performer, played her role to the hilt, and put up a good fight until the end of campaign. Those of us who knew her well, however, could see that the fire was gone, replaced by overwhelming fatigue, frustration, and, ultimately, anger and resentment. After all, her accomplishments were being challenged and disparaged by a markedly unaccomplished man with a famous name.

We got a glimpse of the impact of that anger and resentment early in the campaign. At a huge rally in Texarkana at the end of a long, hot day in August, a mere slip of the tongue put our whole campaign on edge. When she was speaking to her supporters, she referred to Bush as "some jerk who thinks he can be governor!" She tried to walk it back, but too many people—including reporters— had heard the remark. I got a tearful call from her about 10:30 that evening. "I really screwed up," she said. "I knew I wasn't supposed to attack him personally. I don't know what happened. I'm so sorry." It was almost a personal apology to me, as if she had committed the dreadful act of letting down one of her true believers. Although I tried to reassure her, the story was all over the newspapers the next day, and it hurt us decisively. From that moment on, we knew—and so did Karl Rove—that we had probably ceded the high ground in the campaign to George W. Bush. He seized it the very next day, addressing the comment with both humor and self-righteous disdain.

"The last time I was called a jerk was at Sam Houston Elementary School in Midland, Texas. I'm not going to call the governor names," he pledged. "I'm going to elevate this debate to a level where Texans want it."[6]

From the beginning of the campaign, Rove coached Bush to avoid making the kinds of mistakes that Clayton Williams had made against Richards in 1990. "Because Richards predictably benefited from Williams's crass treatment of her, I knew she would try to goad Bush into attacking her . . . so she could be a victim a second time," Rove wrote in his memoir.[7] He advised Bush to avoid letting Richards get under his skin. After her "jerk" comment, it must have been obvious to Rove that it was Bush who had actually gotten under Richards's skin.

Bush's disciplined "niceness" goaded her and our campaign into other mistakes that set the 1994 campaign on a different trajectory than the more focused 1990 contest. We were all over the map on dozens of issues, pointing out her record in ethics and insurance reform and all of the other measures she had undertaken to create the New Texas. The problem was that we got stuck in our own past, and successful campaigns have to be about the future. People don't want to know what you've done for them in the past; they want to know what you're going to do for them in the future. Bush gave voters a vision of the future—plus he had all those suburban demographic shifts on his side.

After the loss, few Democrats outside of our inner circle seemed to realize what might lie ahead. After all, how predictive of the future could Ann Richards's loss really be? Democrats controlled the legislature, the state's highest courts, and most of the other statewide offices too. Richards's appointees were still serving on all those boards and commissions. It would just be a matter of regrouping to win back the governor's office, just as Democrats had managed to do when they defeated Bill Clements in 1982.

Few Democrats at the time seemed to realize that voters in seven huge suburban counties surrounding the largest cities were the key factor in the Republican surge: Collin and Denton counties outside of Dallas and Fort Worth; Brazoria, Montgomery, and Fort Bend counties outside of Houston; Hays and Williamson counties outside of Austin. Republicans canvassed, mailed, and turned out suburban voters in numbers Texas had never seen before, and Democrats were slow in figuring out what they were up against. After Ann lost the election, she used to joke that her economic development initiatives had created all sorts of new jobs. The problem was that the people who came to Texas to fill those jobs had voted against her.

Slow Learners in a Fast-Moving Game

When George W. Bush's reelection bid rolled around in 1998, the last member of the 1982 "Gang of Four" remaining in office decided to take him on.[8] Although it was a long shot, Land Commissioner Garry Mauro had always been a top vote-getter and had drawn particularly heavy Hispanic support in the Rio Grande Valley. He was an original "FOB," or friend of Bill Clinton, who could come to Texas to help generate a heavy Democratic vote in key areas. More importantly, Mauro believed he would have access to Clinton's vast fund-raising network. But the Monica Lewinsky scandal broke during the campaign, the Clintons were busy trying to survive, and Mauro couldn't scratch. He was able to raise only about $3 million to Bush's $30 million, and he lost in a landslide—69 percent to 31 percent. Rove and the Bush team wanted a reelection blowout to demonstrate strength going into the Republican presidential primaries for the 2000 election. They got it.

Yet Democrats still believed that Mauro's loss was just one more aberration, not indicative of a major shift in the state's voting patterns. After all, Mauro was outspent, ten to one, and didn't have enough money to buy TV time or to make a major push to get Hispanic voters to the polls. And Bush's popularity was simply too strong to overcome. The prevailing sentiment among Democrats was that they could take back the governor's office once Bush was gone. "Next time" would become a recurring mantra.

Dream Team Turns Nightmare

In 2002, Texas Democrats put together a "Dream Team," with wealthy Laredo oil man and banker Tony Sanchez Jr. running for governor and the first African American mayor of Dallas, the ebullient Ron Kirk, vying for the U.S. Senate. Sanchez challenged Rick Perry, who as lieutenant governor had moved into the higher office when Bush went to Washington and was now running for his first real term. Kirk was running for an open Senate seat and faced Republican attorney general John Cornyn.

Sanchez put almost $70 million of his own money into the race and was supposed to be the magic man who could inspire the state's Hispanic population to come out in record numbers and restore Democrats to power. But instead of luring voters, Sanchez's money was a magnet for every hungry political consultant in the country. Most of his consultants served him badly. Although he had more campaign money at his disposal than his opponent, Sanchez's resources were so poorly allocated that he was outfoxed by Perry, whose tough-guy Texas Way demeanor stood in stark contrast to the racial and ethnic diversity put forth by the Democrats. Perry proved a formidable match for a well-intentioned candidate with a disorganized campaign. Although Sanchez actually managed to double the Latino turnout from the previous election, it was not enough to overcome the Republican advantage in the suburbs. In 2014, after Sanchez saw the Wendy Davis campaign fall apart, he told a friend that it looked like a mirror image of his own campaign in 2002—ill-served by a bunch of consultants whose ideas did not match the reality of the times.

Once again, in 2006, Democrats tried to bounce back. They were still waiting for the magic Mexican American voters to show up but did not really understand that the Rio Grande Valley was no longer the epicenter of Latino voting strength in Texas. In fact, there were more Hispanic voters in Houston than in the entire Rio Grande Valley. Even though Democrats had been trounced at the highest level in 2002, they barely lost close races for lieutenant governor and comptroller, the state's chief financial officer, with the candidates drawing between 47 and 49 percent of the vote. Maybe Perry might be vulnerable after all. If so, lots of people wanted in on that act.

The 2006 race took on a clownish quality, with independent candidates like Kinky Friedman, who couldn't make up his mind if he was a musician in a band called the Texas Jew Boys or a dog rescuer in Kerr County. Also jumping into the race was former state comptroller Carole Keeton McClellan Rylander Strayhorn, the thrice-married Democrat-turned-Republican-turned-Independent, who at one time or another had used every one of her married names when running for various political offices. In 1998, she had been elected as a Republican to the office of state comptroller but decided that the best way to challenge Governor Perry was to run as an independent. She was the mother of one of George W. Bush's press secretaries at the time, Scott McClellan, but the Bush crowd of consultants, family, and friends stayed out of the race. The Democrat in the four-way race was former congressman Chris Bell.

Bell had run for so many different offices so many different times that he could have been considered one of those perennial ballot-chasers. However, Bell had won enough elections to be considered a legitimate candidate for governor. He had served on the Houston city council in the late 1990s, and had even won a seat in the U.S. House of Representatives in 2002. But like a lot of white Democrats from Texas, Bell soon lost his seat because of Tom DeLay's redistricting maneuvers. Outraged, Bell filed an ethics complaint against DeLay, which caused the House Ethics Committee to "admonish" DeLay for abuse of power and alleged illegal solicitation of money. But Bell couldn't raise enough money from weary Democrats for his own race and drew only about 30 percent of the vote. Of course, the ultimate victor, Rick Perry, didn't exactly wow the voters, either. The bizarre bunch-up of candidates allowed the victorious Perry to get by with only 39 percent of the vote. He looked so vulnerable that Democrats thought that by 2010 they could surely take back "their" state.

For a while, it looked like they might. When Houston's popular mayor Bill White decided to take on Perry, he had the money, the credentials, and a solid base of support in Houston. He had served as deputy secretary of energy during the Clinton administration and had won three mayoral terms in the nonpartisan municipal elections, drawing over 90 percent of the vote for his reelection bids. White had cut property taxes as well as Houston's soaring crime rate. He had drawn national acclaim in 2005 when he opened the city's Astrodome and the George R. Brown Convention Center to thousands of fleeing New Orleans residents who had lost their homes during Hurricane Katrina. What's more, he set up programs to find them jobs, permanent housing, and education opportunities within Houston. His Katrina response won him the prestigious John F. Kennedy Profile in Courage Award in 2007. If anyone had the credentials to become an outstanding governor of Texas, it would have been Bill White. He just lacked a few key attributes.

White had the kind of personality that could lower the energy wattage rather than light up a room when he entered. Yet he had such a strong sense of himself that he knew exactly what he wanted in his campaign—down to the last trivial detail—not necessarily a good trait in a statewide candidate. He also seemed to believe that his strong municipal performance would translate into a turnout of Houston voters heavy enough to cancel out Republican gains in the suburbs ringing Dallas. But like most unsuccessful ventures, the White campaign made a key erroneous assumption: that Governor Rick Perry was vulnerable. In fact, he was a ferocious campaigner who would let nothing stand in his way to victory.

Perry outspent White three to one and dumped so much money into Houston in the final weeks of the campaign that he destroyed White's hometown advantage and the base vote he had counted on. White drew 43 percent of the statewide vote to Perry's almost 55 percent.

This time the Texas Democratic Party finally realized that the fix was in. The Tea Party was driving national politics, and at home, Republicans were morphing into clowns, crackpots, and Christian crusaders.

SEVEN

Clowns, Crackpots, and Christian Crusaders

ALTHOUGH DEMOCRATS LOVE TO BLAME
the Tea Party for every outbreak of irrational behavior among Republicans, the kinds of craziness that capture headlines today actually began back in the 1980s—when Texas Democrats still held
power. It all started with the public schools, a perennial target for
right-wing Christian crusaders.

In his successful 1982 race to unseat Bill Clements as governor, Democrat Mark White's major issue was the improvement
of Texas public schools. His first act as governor was to appoint a
special commission to come up with recommendations to upgrade
every aspect of Texas's education system, which had not seen an
overhaul in policies or procedures since the 1940s. Because of Ross
Perot's role in building a knowledge-based economy for the state,
White appointed him to head the commission. Perot brought

along his legal counsel, Tom Luce, to be chief of staff for the Texas Select Committee on Public Education.

The yearlong effort—one of the first public school reform efforts in the nation—put Luce at the thorny center of policy making and political intrigue. The committee plunged into controversy almost immediately when its research established a link between Texas's obsession with high school football and the poor academic preparedness of its graduates. Although there were numerous recommendations to improve Texas schools, it was the famous "No Pass, No Play" edict that stuck. If a high school student failed even one course during a six-week grading period, he or she would be ineligible to play any sport or participate in marching band or any other district or statewide competition. The move sent coaches, school board members, and parents into a frenzy. But it was another provision of education reform that gave Tom Luce his first brush with the state's ultra-right-wing elements that would ultimately take over his party.

One of the recommendations of the Select Committee on Public Education was to require local school districts to provide kindergarten for poor children who qualified for free instruction under Title I of the Elementary and Secondary Education Act, passed in 1965 under President Lyndon Johnson. Although Texas school districts would be mandated to provide these kindergarten programs, participation of parents and children would be optional, if the legislature adopted the committee's recommendations. In other words, there would be no compulsory attendance for preschool-age children. However, when the recommendations were published, talk radio exploded, with fundamentalist Christian preachers telling parents that Texas was going to take their young children away and indoctrinate them against God and family.

Christian talk radio had become a staple of Texas political life in the 1970s, an outgrowth of the rise of the fundamentalist and evangelical movements that stretched from California throughout the Sun Belt. Dallas and Houston were home to nondenominational megachurches, largely white enclaves that had up to 20,000 members. The religious right—then and now—covers a broad spectrum of belief, ranging from those who believe in the Rapture and biblical inerrancy to those who embrace a prosperity Gospel or those who practice speaking in tongues. Because most fundamentalists and evangelicals were also social conservatives, the Republican Party had made a concerted effort to turn all of those believers into a reliable voting bloc. Their power within the Republican Party picked up steam after Reagan's election in 1980. And Tom Luce got to see it, up close and personal, on an issue that was supremely important to him.

The Education of Tom Luce

What began as an nonpartisan effort to improve educational outcomes in Texas ended, Luce recalled, with a thousand inflamed parents from Bible-beating churches all across the state massing on the Capitol steps. After rousing speeches the crowd streamed inside the building to persuade individual lawmakers to vote against the public school reform proposals. It was a frightening experience for Luce, who thought these religious zealots were going to destroy everything he had accomplished that year. Working well into the night, he and other supporters of the bill were able to mobilize public school advocates and community groups to come to Austin for a counter-lobbying effort. Although the school bill ultimately prevailed, thanks to a coalition of Democrats and reform-minded Republicans, the battle set a tone that began to reflect the growing influence of conservative Christians within the Republican Party. Still, Luce got his first taste of state-level politics and now had a reputation as an effective leader who could pass complicated legislation by unifying diverse constituencies. In late 1989, he decided he wanted to run for governor.

Luce remembers that when he told then–state treasurer Ann Richards what he wanted to do, Richards joked that he was much too nice and that his fellow Republicans would "eat him alive," as he recalls. Luce finished a distant third in the six-person primary that nominated the loose-lipped Clayton Williams. Afterward, Luce ran into Richards, who by then had survived her own party's brutal primary to become the Democratic nominee for governor. She gave Luce a big hug and whispered in his ear, "See, I told you so."

Ann Richards's prophecy came back to haunt her within four years, as George W. Bush and his crowd ate *her* alive. By then, the Christian right was a key factor in her loss to Bush. She and Luce got singed by the same religious fire.

Luce stayed active in Republican politics during George W. Bush's tenure as governor and became a major supporter of Bush's ongoing venture into school reform. With the help of Democrats who had fallen for the Bush charm offensive, the Texas legislature enacted a rather draconian accountability system for the public schools and made Texas one of the first states in the nation to introduce high-stakes testing, developed and scored by private testing firms. Later, those firms would be endorsed by federal law and become billion-dollar businesses under Bush's No Child Left Behind Act. Luce believed, along with Bush, that testing and accountability were essential to raising the level of public education. His role in trying to improve the nation's schools shaped the remainder of his career. In 2005, President Bush appointed Tom Luce assistant secretary of education.

While Luce was away in Washington and Bush was embroiling the nation in dual wars in Afghanistan and Iraq, the Texas Republican Party was changing. By the time Luce returned to Texas in 2008, he and many of his generation were well on their way to becoming an endangered species within the party they helped build.

The Political Genius of Rick Perry—Really!

Although he rarely exhibited it on the national scene, Rick Perry may have been the most tactical and powerful politician Texas has produced since Lyndon Johnson. He had an instinct for power and knew how to use it—rewarding his friends and punishing his enemies. While the practice is not uncommon in politics, Perry is reported to have carried it to the extreme, embodying what critics called an "insider pay to play culture."[1] According to a *New York Times* analysis, clients of his friend and former chief of staff–turned-lobbyist Mike Toomey ended up winning almost $2 billion in state contracts after 2008 when Toomey left the governor's office.[2] And it was widely known around the Capitol that a respected lobbyist for the Texas Medical Association had lost his job after he publicly criticized Perry's veto of legislation that physicians had supported.[3] While most Texas voters paid little attention to the inner workings of the governor's office, they did pay attention when Perry famously seized credit for Texas's booming economy in the early 2000s, though it was largely the result of soaring oil prices. When he ran television spots bragging that Texas was "open for business," he appealed to the pride of Texas voters who wanted to believe that Texas was simply the best place to live and conduct business without government interference.

Perry, always a step or two ahead of a coming political trend, had been one of the early switchers when he left the Democratic Party to become a Republican in 1989. Yet Perry was not always the blustery right-wing ideologue he later appeared to be. In the Texas legislature, Perry had been one of the "Pit Bull" Democrats who understood the role that technology could play in increasing efficiency for state agencies. He was willing to invest state money and resources to make it happen. While Ann Richards was treasurer, Perry became a valuable ally in securing funding to upgrade computers and check-processing systems and for investment opportunities that were designed to streamline Texas's "green eyeshade" days of careless money management.[4]

This pragmatic support continued even after his party swap. When he became lieutenant governor, Perry was quite willing to use state funds to back new technology and entrepreneurial ventures. When I was CEO of KLRU-TV, the PBS station in Austin, Rick Perry was instrumental in helping all 13 Texas PBS stations get $22 million in state money for the FCC-required conversion to digital technology—the first, and only, state funding that Texas public television stations ever received. In his first few years as governor, Perry gave every appearance of being little more than a conventional business-oriented Republican who was always will-ing to help his cronies get a good deal from the state.

Then in 2008, Barack Hussein Obama was elected president of the United States, and everything changed.

Many Texans already believed that Democrats were social-ists, atheists, sexual libertines, and heedless redistributors of hard-working taxpayers' money to unworthy slackers and black welfare queens—the enduring legacy of Ronald Reagan's rhetoric. The election of an African American to the presidency awakened an old racist strain that had long been an undercurrent in right-wing circles in Texas. Once again—just like after the Civil War, when blacks claimed seats in the Texas legislature and in local communi-ties during Reconstruction—for some, seeing a black man in office rekindled a belief that the natural order of things had been up-ended. And here, too, Rick Perry understood the implications for Texas politics long before anyone else.

Three months after Obama's inauguration, Governor Perry made a speech that signaled to the nation that something different was happening in Texas. In April 2009, he spoke to a gathering of over a thousand Republican Party activists and revved up the crowd by saying, "I'm not sure you're a bunch of right-wing extremists. But if you are, I'm with you! 'Cause you are a true patriot today in this country." As the crowd burst into applause, Perry praised them as "individuals who embrace concepts like lower taxes and smaller government and freedom for every individual. I'm talking about states' rights, about states' rights!"[5]

After the speech, a reporter asked him if he was threatening secession, and Perry took the bait. "If Washington continues to thumb their nose at the American people, who knows what might come out of that?"[6] Perry touched a raw nerve that had festered for years in some parts of Texas. The emotional experience of thinking your power is secure and then seeing it threatened—or at least imagining that it is being threatened—was the catalyst for the wild secession talk that Perry encouraged. Yes, its roots are racist. But it also goes beyond racism. Resentment against the federal government was embedded in some deep collective Texas psyche. The proof? More than 116,000 people signed a petition on the White House website requesting peaceful separation of Texas from the United States. Some signed it as a joke or a protest, but a few were dead serious. One Republican county official in East Texas said that his neighbors were coming to appreciate that "the fundamental cultural differences between Texas and other parts of the United States may be best addressed by an amicable divorce, a peaceful separation."[7]

While many Americans across the nation may have muttered "good riddance" at the prospect of secession, Perry's remarks threw open the doors to the kind of hyperbolic, hate-filled public rhetoric that had been shunned by most mainstream Republicans in Texas after the Kennedy assassination. Although Bill Clements had used social issues like abortion and even racist code words to talk about school busing and welfare cheats, this was different.

SMU political scientist Cal Jillson recalled a phrase that found broad currency in Texas after the Civil War, when white Texans viewed the very idea of black equality as implicitly humiliating. "They could not conceive how blacks could rise if whites did not fall. 'How could the bottom rail be on top,' in the phrase of the day, 'unless the top rail went to the bottom?'"[8] With Obama's election, many Republicans saw the bottom rail on top and felt as if they stood to lose everything they valued. When people are faced with loss, real or perceived, irrational panic sets in. This panic was by no means limited to Texas; with the rise of the Tea Party movement, it spread all over the country. It just seemed a little more virulent here.

Ezra Klein, a liberal blogger and columnist, has dubbed the extreme reaction to the nation's first black president "Obama Derangement Syndrome." Conservative columnist Charles Krauthammer had first applied the term "Bush Derangement Syndrome" to describe what he believed to be the response of liberal Democrats to George W. Bush's invasion of Iraq in 2003. But liberals' reaction was to Bush's policies. The Republican rejection of President Obama, Klein notes, has been more about his "person," reflecting "paranoia about the man himself, that he is, in some fundamental way, different, foreign, untrustworthy, even traitorous."[9]

Against a backdrop of changing political rhetoric, it was Perry's decisive defeat of popular U.S. senator Kay Bailey Hutchison in the 2010 Republican gubernatorial primary that emboldened right-wingers and states-righters to take on their own moderate Republican officeholders.

The Confrontation

In 2010 Kay Bailey Hutchison was Texas's most popular politician—Republican or Democrat. In the little-noticed Republican breakthrough at the time, she had been elected state treasurer in 1990 when Ann Richards vacated that office. Thanks to this twist of fate, Hutchison and Perry won high-level state offices at the same time, and it would be he who ultimately ended her political career.

Hutchison continued Richards's efforts to modernize the treasury, and except for a Democratic district attorney's overzealous indictment of her on official misconduct charges relating to handling of public records and the subsequent toss of the charges, she had a sterling reputation among Texans.

As a young TV reporter for KHOU in Houston, Kay Bailey was a protégée of Anne Armstrong, part of the great South Texas ranching family that had bolted the Democrats along with other Texas Regulars in 1948. In 1972, Bailey was part of the first wave of Republican lawmakers to serve in the Texas House of Representatives. Always supportive of women's rights, she worked well with her Democratic colleagues. Texas politics at the time had a rather cozy, familial feel, particularly within the Republican Party. In 1978, Bailey married state party chair Ray Hutchison, whom she had met in Austin when he was a representative from Dallas. She added his surname and became a partner in one of the state's premier power couples.

In 1993, when Lloyd Bentsen vacated his U.S. Senate seat to accept President Bill Clinton's offer to become secretary of the treasury, Governor Richards appointed former U.S. congressman Robert Krueger to serve until a special election to fill the post could be set. Republicans, already convinced that their time was nigh, saw the open seat as prime opportunity and set out to recruit Kay Bailey Hutchison to enter the race.

"I always had my eye on the governor's office," she said, recalling her initial hesitation about making a Senate run.[10] Private polls showing her as the Republican most likely to win ultimately persuaded her to enter the race. Ann Richards knew that if Hutchison ran, Texas Democrats could lose that Senate seat forever to the popular Republican. Yet Richards had a hard time settling on an alternative when she made the temporary appointment to fill the vacancy. She wanted to pick someone who could win the special election. One popular state official she considered was not pro-choice enough for her liking. She heard rumors about the womanizing proclivities of another favorite. And the woman she would have liked to appoint—Lena Guerrero—had already been discredited because she had falsely listed on her résumé that she was a Phi Beta Kappa graduate of the University of Texas, when she held neither that distinction nor a diploma. So Richards settled on Krueger, the patrician former dean of arts and sciences at Duke University.

Krueger had recently been elected statewide to the Texas Railroad Commission, which regulates oil and gas production, and had once made an unsuccessful run for the U.S. Senate. Unfortunately, Krueger turned out to be the weakest of all possible candidates. The special election drew a field of 24 hopefuls, and Hutchison and Krueger finished at the top, each with about 29 percent of the vote. In the runoff election, she easily defeated the professorial Krueger, who ran the kind of clueless, out-of-touch-with-Texas campaign that would soon become the norm among Texas Democrats. Hutchison won 67.3 percent of the vote to Krueger's dismal 32.7 percent. While it was hard to lose Bentsen's Senate seat to a Republican, few Democrats paused to consider that Krueger's percentage of the vote might represent the true, shrinking Democratic base strength against a well-financed, popular Republican. And like other Democrats preparing for Ann Richards's reelection bid the following year, I myself did not waste a minute thinking that the best a Democrat might do in an increasingly Republican-leaning state would be to win barely one-third of the vote in a straight-up contest with a strong Republican contender.

Republican operative Wayne Thorburn believed that Hutchison's election was the beginning of the transition to Republican dominance in statewide politics.[11] Republicans have held both U.S. Senate seats since then.

Hutchison rose to leadership positions in the U.S. Senate during her three terms. Although she was staunchly pro-life, she was also an advocate for women's health, pay equity, and equal rights for women. Texas women—both Democratic and Republican—recognized her as a friend. Hutchison never invoked the kind of slash-and-burn rhetoric that was becoming the norm in her party.

Hutchison had built a solid reputation as a senator who got things done for her state. She was a major supporter of the Texas oil and gas industry, which gave her more money than any other member in the Senate. What got her into trouble in the race for governor against Rick Perry were the very accomplishments she had worked hardest to achieve: bringing hundreds of millions of dollars to Texas for special projects. She was a champion of causes as diverse as Houston's Space Center and water and sewer improvement ventures for poverty-stricken Mexican American communities along the border. She also obtained federal funds to renovate an historic art deco building in Dallas to house a women's history museum. Almost every community could list some special project secured by Hutchison's savvy.

By 2010, Hutchison longed to come back home to Texas. She and Ray had adopted two young children, and she wanted to be able to spend more time with them. She hoped that life in the governor's mansion might provide a more normal family routine. She began to prepare her run for the office she had always wanted. Early polls showed her trouncing the incumbent Perry, who had barely won 39 percent of the vote in that bizarre four-way general election race in 2006. But Rick Perry was a survivor. He had won every race he had ever run since he first entered politics in the early 1980s. After the popular Democratic state comptroller John Sharp lost a close race for lieutenant governor against Perry in 1998, he complained, "Running against Perry is like running against God. Everything breaks his way. Either he's the luckiest guy in the world or the Lord is taking care of him."[12]

Riding the dominant right-wing wave among Republicans in 2010, Perry made things break his way. He wrapped Hutchison's estimable Senate record around her neck and pulled the cord tighter as his campaign rhetoric reached a fever pitch. She was a Washington insider. She was a pork-barrel liberal. She was a big spender. She was an elitist backer of Wall Street bailouts. He even started calling her "Kay Bailout Hutchison."

Going into the primary, it didn't matter to Tea Partiers that Hutchison had the endorsements and full support of the venerable Republican leader Peter O'Donnell, who was now one of the biggest philanthropists in Texas. She had all of the old Bush team on her side—Karl Rove, former vice president Dick Cheney, former secretary of state James Baker, and even the first President Bush. But none of them had the power or draw of Rick Perry.

Hutchison's staff was slow to respond to Perry's charges and didn't know how to campaign in a political environment that was so decidedly anti-Washington. When it slowly dawned on them that the Tea Party was now the strongest faction within the Republican base, they made a strategic error by trying to turn the elegant, lady-like Hutchison into Rick Perry in a skirt. But there's no room to run to the right of a right-winger; as one Republican campaign operative observed, "You just have to point out how batshit crazy they are." But Hutchison's staff convinced her to run to the right. The move made her seem inauthentic and uncomfortable throughout the race. Insiders believe that she lost control of her own campaign and regretted that she allowed herself to become the captive of her own consultants.

Perry emerged victorious once again, beating Hutchison 51 percent to 30 percent. Establishment Republicans experienced the same despair and disheartenment after Hutchison's loss that Democrats felt after Richards lost to George W. Bush in 1994.

The election sent a clear signal that moderate Republican incumbents would be vulnerable to challenges from outsider candidates who had the guts to take them on. "I think the message is pretty clear," Perry told supporters at his victory party on election night. "Conservatism has never been stronger than it is today, and we are taking our country back."[13]

In 2012, Ted Cruz became the first candidate for a major office since Perry to capitalize on the hard rightward shift that was taking place in the party, and he surprised moderate Republicans in their primary once again when he defeated the independently wealthy lieutenant governor David Dewhurst for the U.S. Senate nomination. Establishment Republicans seemed to be in the same kind of denial about the reality of their situation that Democrats experienced after Ann Richard's loss in 1994. But reality was hard to ignore after Cruz's victory. Right-wing extremist candidates began to take on pragmatic Republicans who served in local offices as well as in the Texas legislature. And the incumbents couldn't quite figure out how to combat their challengers. They were like those hapless Democrats who kept running losing campaigns in the decades after Ann Richards lost. They ran mediocre, lackluster campaigns in old, traditional ways, and allowed a horde of crackpots and clowns to sweep into office.

In 2014, the party took an even more marked turn to the right by defeating Wendy Davis and filling the top three offices in the state. Governor Greg Abbott, Lieutenant Governor Dan Patrick, and Attorney General Ken Paxton were the most extreme right-wing officeholders Texas had ever seen. In that same election, 30 new Tea Party Republicans were elected to the state house of representatives. Members of the 2015 legislative session sounded like a bunch of Rush Limbaugh "ditto-heads," echoing the most nonsensical outbursts of the right-wing talk show host. Dan Patrick led the pack, telling one group of supporters who wanted to make sure Texas never allowed gay marriage, "It's not federal government's business to tell Texans what to do in Texas on any issue. So it's a fight worth fighting for." Newly elected state representative Cecil Bell told the same crowd that he would attempt to stop state and local officials from issuing marriage licenses to gay and lesbian couples because "God is right, and God is sovereign. And in Texas, we are going to stand up for those traditional values."[14]

Even after the June 26, 2015, historic Supreme Court decision prohibiting states from banning same-sex marriages, Texas officials remained defiant. Ken Paxton called the court's actions a "lawless decision" and advised county clerks that they did not have to issue marriage licenses to gay couples if doing so violated their religious beliefs.[15] Governor Abbott condemned the court action as well. "Five justices on the Supreme Court have imposed on the entire country their personal views on an issue that the Constitution and the court's previous decisions reserve to the people of the states," he charged.[16]

But members of the Texas legislature, meeting for four months in the spring of 2015, seemed even nuttier on a whole range of Tea Party issues. New representative Jonathan Strickland put a sign on his door identifying himself a former "pre-born fetus," a sentiment shared by many of the new legislators who believed that a fetus had greater constitutional rights than the mother who carried it in her womb.

If any Tea Party member anywhere objected to any perceived restriction on individual freedom, even in the name of an overall public good, one of their yahoo legislators responded with proposals for new laws.

Freshman state senator Don Huffines from Dallas, who had defeated a moderate Republican in the primary, proposed allowing the legislature to retroactively veto local decisions by cities whenever it wanted—particularly if localities ventured into areas of gay rights, living-wage ordinances, or even banning the use of plastic bags at grocery stores. Other legislators proposed bills to prevent municipalities from installing cameras at busy intersections to catch drivers who ran red lights, which supposedly was an infringement on individual liberty. One proposal would have prevented cities from putting voter initiatives on the ballot without prior approval from Austin. The anti-government lunacy struck at the heart of Texas's 100 years of home-rule tradition that allowed cities to respond to local needs without state interference.

Political columnist Richard Parker described members of the legislature as "Big Government Republicans" who engaged in a power grab to diminish the voting strength of urban Texans.[17] Beneath the lunacy, however, were reasons for the anti-city madness.

It is no secret that the core Democratic Party base is located in those very cities that many of the proposed bills would have adversely affected, and most of the proposed restrictions on local governments were aimed at Texas's most progressive communities. Fortunately for Texas cities, most of these proposals died in the legislative logjams that usually occur in the final days of the session. However, this being Texas, the elimination of the state's few remaining paltry restrictions on guns in public places faced no such hurdles. Gun owners were given free rein to openly carry their firearms any place they wanted—shopping centers, restaurants, grocery stores, public parks, and even on college campuses—much to the consternation of protesting college presidents and law enforcement officials. But NRA-backed Governor Abbott proudly signed the gun bills at a local firing range.

As all of this was playing out, the true architect of the current Republican Party in Texas was keeping score on key votes to put together his enemies list for the next go-round of primary elections. His vengeful tactics would make even Karl Rove seem timid.

The Punisher

Right-wing zealot Michael Quinn Sullivan is the unofficial Republican political boss of the clowns, crackpots, and Christian crusaders who now rule Texas. And he has become the "punisher" of any pragmatic Republican who departs from his ultraright party line. Sullivan has the fierce tenacity of NRA leader Wayne LaPierre, the vengeful bluster of anti-taxer Grover Norquist, and the money of the infamous Koch brothers. The combination is one of the factors that have sent the Texas Republican Party into a frenzy of irrational craziness.

Sullivan's organizations, with the help of right-wing think tanks, have created a new kind of hyperpartisan officeholder that has led the party further to the right with each succeeding election. The Sullivan Republicans are anti-government, anti-tax, anti-abortion, anti-gay, anti-immigration, and anti-separation of church and state. They advocate creationism and censorship of the state's school textbooks, which have in some cases wiped African American leaders and progressives off the pages of American history.

Sullivan, who had a rather undistinguished career as a reporter for a couple of small-town newspapers, ached for the big time and joined the staff of Congressman Ron Paul in 1995 as press secretary. By 2001, he had become the media director of the Texas Public Policy Foundation in Austin, a nonprofit think tank far to the right of the Heritage Foundation and other national Republican policy groups. San Antonio medical equipment entrepreneur Dr. James Leininger, a Republican, founded the group in 1989. Leininger's original cause was support of public school vouchers; over time the group expanded its agenda and influence. Today, the foundation has on its payroll a group of academic and ex-officeholder "fellows," a staff of about a dozen, and a budget of $8 million to $10 million annually. It issues white papers with the finesse of the Heritage Foundation and is a regular contributor of op-ed pieces in Texas newspapers, as well as detailed, scholarly looking reports against Medicare, Medicaid, Social Security, and the ill effects of minimum wage increases. Its stated principles are liberty, personal responsibility, private property rights, free markets, and limited government. But whose liberties are they most interested in protecting?

The Texas Observer reported that the group was "flush with donations from the likes of the Koch brothers, ExxonMobil, Altria (tobacco), GEO Group (private prisons) and dozens of other corporations, interest groups, right-wing foundations and wealthy businessmen with an agenda to promote."[18] Craig McDonald, director of the liberal watchdog group Texans for Public Justice, charged that Leininger's group's donors are a "Who's Who of Texas polluters, giant utilities, and big insurance companies."[19] The group has close ties to the American Legislative Exchange Council and has gotten its friends in the legislature to sponsor more than two dozen pieces of "model" legislation on everything from opposing Obamacare to eliminating Texas's meager environmental protection laws to attacking renewable energy and denying climate change.

In 2006, it spawned two groups headed by Michael Quinn Sullivan: Empower Texas and Texans for Fiscal Responsibility. Because these groups have a 501(c)(3) designation under the tax code, donors are able to deduct their contributions—even though the organizations often push the limits of the law in their support of or opposition to candidates in Republican primaries and general elections. Sullivan's groups have opposed establishment conservatives like Kay Bailey Hutchison, David Dewhurst, and more than a dozen pragmatic Republicans in the Texas state house. The group claims credit for defeating every single one of them. One of those ousted conservative Republicans described Sullivan as "pure evil"—so evil, in fact, that a small pushback against his influence may be growing.

After attempting a takedown of Republican house Speaker Joe Straus at the beginning of the 2015 legislative session, Sullivan's crackpots could draw only 19 votes against Straus's coalition of pragmatic Republicans and Democrats who joined together to save him. Sullivan vowed to hunt down and punish any Republican who voted for Straus. Upon reelection, Straus, who is from a wealthy political family in San Antonio, proclaimed that neither he nor his followers would be intimidated by Sullivan any longer.[20] Although Straus managed to block some of the craziest pieces of Tea Party legislation, enough of those laws got through to keep Texas tilting further to the right. But Straus's declaration of independence from Sullivan's threats apparently has not been enough to reassure almost a dozen Republican house and senate members who have decided not to seek reelection in order to avoid a primary election slugfest with Sullivan's candidates in 2016.

Longtime moderate Republicans like Tom Luce have been dismayed by the power of Sullivan and the extreme rightward turn in the party they helped build. Maybe the term "moderate" is a misnomer. Although about 30 percent of Texas Republicans do not fall into the crazy right-wing end of their party's spectrum, they are not necessarily moderate. Former senator Hutchison bristles at the term and still proclaims her allegiance to traditional Republican principles. "I am a conservative," she insists.

Perhaps Hutchison has a point. According to Peter Wehner, who served in three Republican presidential administrations and is a senior fellow at the Ethics and Public Policy Center, what today passes for conservatism, as embraced by the most radical elements of the Republican Party, is really a cynical populism. It warns of apocalypse if its prescriptions are not followed and encourages its adherents to believe that they are living under tyranny as long as Democrats—or moderate Republicans—remain in power. It is a decidedly unrealistic view of the world.

True conservatism, on the other hand, "is rooted in human experience," argues Wehner. "It appreciates the complexity of human society . . . it leaves itself open for things empirical, for facts that can lead us to better apprehend the truth."[21] This is not the case among the Republicans who hold power in Texas today, and it is one reason why true conservatives like Hutchison can no longer win her party's nomination.

Tom Luce still finds it hard to believe that a respected conservative leader like Hutchison lost to Perry or that in 2014 Dallas Republican Dan Branch—who had strong backing from the business community and was one of those lawmakers who understood the complexities of human society—lost the Republican nomination for attorney general to hard-right candidate Ken Paxton, who had been under investigation for securities law violations at the time. Six months after he took office, Paxton was indicted on three felony securities counts, confirming the worst fears of establishment Republicans.[22]

"When I looked at the primary turnout numbers, the winner got only got 3.5 percent of the vote that Republicans usually pull in a general election," Luce recalled. "That means that some 3.5 percent of the voters, the hard right of the Republican Party who control the primaries, also now control the state of Texas." Luce's analysis was right on target. For the past 20 years, any Republican running statewide—including one under criminal investigation— could beat any Democrat on the ballot. Controlling the Republican primaries now equates with controlling the apparatus of Texas government.

That may ultimately be the party's undoing.

Leaks in the Big Red Bubble

Since 2010, Republican leaders have bragged about the great "Texas Miracle" of job growth that managed to lead the way during the slow economic recovery from the Great Recession. Texas created more jobs than any other state in the nation, largely based on the booming energy sector but also on a surge in manufacturing. There is no denying that many businesses thrive in the Texas climate of low taxes and high business subsidies, low wages and lax regulations, and protective tort claim laws that shield them from their mistakes or malfeasance. But just like in the old oil-boom days when wealth flowed to a handful of people, the state as a whole has not benefited from the prosperity that has accrued to many of its individual residents. State spending on essential government services, particularly Texas's sprawling public school system, has not kept pace with inflation.

Not since Ann Richards's days in office has Texas invested a significant amount of its vast resources in its own people. When former governor Rick Perry or U.S. Senator Ted Cruz brag about the great Texas economic miracle, they don't mention the fact that Texas leads the nation in child poverty rates or that Texas has the highest percentage of people without health insurance in the nation—even after passage of the Affordable Care Act. More

Texas workers are injured or die on the job because of unsafe work-ing conditions than in any state in the union. Further, Texas has the weakest workers' compensation system for employees who are injured or killed because many Texas businesses are no longer re-quired to have workers' compensation insurance. Individuals are left to their own devices and must seek out lawyers who will take their cases. Similar easing of regulatory measures has resulted in Texas leading the nation in carbon emissions, the critical measure affecting global climate change. Texas highways are crumbling be-cause of neglected repairs, and its state pensions are underfunded. Texas spends less per pupil in its schools than 39 other states. It has the highest school dropout rate and the highest teen preg-nancy rate in the country. Texas has such restrictive abortion laws that it has mandated the closure of all but a handful of women's health clinics that had provided cancer screenings, mammograms, and contraceptive services for women who don't have private in-surance or access to other forms of health care. Of course, Texas has also refused to comply with the Medicaid expansion program under the Affordable Care Act, which might remedy some of these problems.

What we have in Texas today is the detritus of 20 years of Republican rule. In their public remarks, Representative Louie Gohmert of East Texas and state senator Charles Perry (no re-lation to Rick Perry) of West Texas give a clear picture of the mind-set that has come to dominate among Texas Republicans. Their rhetoric is rooted in conservative religious terminology, even though it is decisively political. Gohmert blamed the mass movie shooting in Aurora, Colorado, in 2012 on liberal attacks on Judeo-Christian beliefs and the rise of a permissive culture that gave rights to gays.[23] And when he was first sworn into office, Charles Perry, who defeated a moderate Republican in the primary before knocking off his Democratic opponent in the general election, claimed the Obama administration was trying to block religion, just as the Nazis did with the Holocaust: "Is it not the same when our government continues to perpetuate laws that lead citizens away from God? The only difference is that the fraud of the Germans was more immediate and whereas the fraud of today's government will not be exposed until the final days and will have eternal-lasting effects," he said.[24]

Texas's long-dominant oil and gas power brokers also benefited from the off-the-wall rhetoric that flows from Republican officials. Their voices ring loud and clear through members of Congress like Representative Joe Barton. In a congressional hearing immediately after the 2010 BP oil spill in the Gulf of Mexico—the worst oil spill in the nation's history—Barton publicly apologized to BP for the federal government's attempts to force the oil driller to take responsibility and pay for damages for its negligence and recklessness in the Gulf.

The funny thing is that oil could bring the whole Republican shebang in Texas to a screeching halt. Every time there is a drop in oil prices, a Texas worker loses a job. According to a model used by the Federal Reserve Bank of Dallas, a drop of about 50 percent in oil prices is associated with a 1.2 percent drop in Texas employment. Based on major layoffs announced in early 2015 by three of Houston's biggest energy and oil service companies—Schlumberger, Halliburton, and Baker Hughes, as well as many smaller companies—Texas could lose about 140,000 energy-related jobs in 2015.[25] It's not just the roughneck in the fields who loses a job; it's the geologist and petroleum engineer in the office, the CPA who keeps the books, the trucker who drives the oil tanker, and the clerk at the convenience store across the street.

In 2015 a drop below the benchmark of $50 a barrel produced a slowdown in the state's booming economy, which had been fueled by $100-a-barrel oil for the past few years. The Texas Miracle was built on high energy prices more than anything that Republicans did to promote the economy. In 2015, no new drilling occurred in the gas-rich West Texas fields, and many of the workers from Ohio or North Carolina who flocked there have gone back home.

The irony is that with all of the favored treatment given to oil companies over the years, the Texas state budget is still heavily dependent on about $3.6 billion in oil and gas severance taxes that are levied when nonrenewable natural resources are extracted from the ground.[26] Less oil taken from the ground means less money coming to the state treasury. Yet the 2015 Republican-controlled Texas legislature based its $209.4 billion biennial budget partly on continued high oil and gas production levels, despite warnings from industry groups that the levels might not be sustainable. What Republicans seem to have overlooked in their political calculations is that when the bottom drops out of oil prices, it tends to leave incumbent officeholders high and dry. Just look back a few years to the impact of oil prices on Texas elections.

Between January 1981 and January 1983, oil prices dropped from almost $104 a barrel to just under $76. Texas's unemployment rate soared from 5.3 percent to 8.4 percent. It brought on a recession and Bill Clements lost his 1982 reelection bid.

While other factors were certainly in play, Clements was able to reclaim the governor's office in 1986, thanks to a drop in the price of oil under Mark White's watch, this time from just over $57 a barrel to just under $40. The Texas unemployment rate rose from 6.4 percent to 9.1 percent.

Although Clements did not run again in 1990, the Republicans could not hold on to the governor's office. Oil prices had stabilized at very low levels, averaging $40.59 a barrel. The Texas unemployment rate remained high, averaging 6.8 percent. And Ann Richards was elected governor.

During Ann Richards's term oil dropped to $24.42 a barrel in January 1994. The unemployment rate remained high at 6.8 percent. Once again, Texans rejected the incumbent governor and elected George W. Bush.

Rick Perry had all the luck, once again. During his three terms as governor, the price of oil kept rising and the Texas unemployment rate rarely inched above 5 percent. The booming energy economy was one reason for Perry's continuing popularity.

By the time of the 2014 election, in which Republican Greg Abbott trounced Democrat Wendy Davis, oil was almost $100 a barrel and the unemployment rate was 5.7 percent, among the lowest of any state in the nation. Predictably, voters did not make a change in the party in power.[27]

So while other factors in Texas statewide elections certainly make a difference, the price of Texas crude, which sets the benchmark worldwide, helps create an economic atmosphere that influences voters. Whatever the price of oil turns out to be the next time Election Day rolls around, Democrats should certainly figure it into their calculations and strategy to rein in the crackpots and crazies who are wreaking havoc in Texas today.

EIGHT

Hispanics– Hype and Hope

WHEN GEORGE W. BUSH WON A SECOND TERM as governor in 1998, he got 46 percent of the Hispanic vote. Democrats thought it was a wild aberration. Maybe it was the Bush name or the Bush charm. But maybe it was something more. Another clue appeared in 2006, when the Democratic candidate for governor, former congressman Chris Bell, pulled only 41 percent of the Hispanic vote in that strange multi-candidate race against Rick Perry. Obviously, simply having the Democratic label by your name was not a draw for the majority of Hispanic voters in that election. You'd think Democrats would have noticed.

Every time the GOP has gotten more than 40 percent of the total Hispanic vote, my Democratic friends have been really surprised. But since the 2014 election debacle, they have to come to terms with the fact that Texas Republicans have a tradition of fighting for every Hispanic vote they can get.

Although the majority of Texas's 3.8 million eligible Latino voters have not deserted the Democratic Party, their loyalty is not automatic. That's a hard fact to absorb. Democrats can't place all their hopes for a big, blue resurgence into some sort of fiesta piñata, just waiting for the right candidate to swing hard enough to burst it open and spill enough Hispanic votes for a big victory party.

The waiting game for an automatic demographic deliverance has not worked. Nor have recent outreach efforts been broad or deep enough to turn out the high numbers of Hispanic voters that Democrats need to expand their base. According to a poll commissioned by America's Voice, which advocates immigration reform, only 25 percent of Texas Latino voters said they were contacted by campaigns encouraging them to vote in the 2012 elections. "That's really abysmal," says Dr. Sylvia Manzano, senior analyst for Latino Decisions, a group that monitors Hispanic politics. "If they're not even getting contacted, then we can only surmise that the less-frequent voters and the eligible-but-not-registered are also not being encouraged to participate."[1]

Since George W. Bush was governor, smart Republicans have stepped up their efforts to make inroads with Latino voters to maintain their grip on Texas. Dumb Republicans seem to be doing everything they can to prevent it, judging by the racist tone of their anti-immigrant rants. Yet overall, pragmatic Republicans realize they have to keep chipping away at Hispanic Democratic vote margins to enhance their chances of staying in power.

The last Texas Democrat running for governor to pull 70 percent of the Hispanic vote was Ann Richards in 1994. Because the state's dynamics have changed so dramatically since then, it's unlikely that a Democrat can reach that peak again. Texas is not Colorado or Nevada, where the Hispanic Democratic vote in presidential elections has soared to 70 percent or higher. Until recently there have been so few Hispanics in those states that Republicans never bothered to target them, and there is simply no history of Latinos voting Republican, as many do in Texas. Unlike their California counterparts, Texas Mexican Americans have never experienced a "Pete Wilson moment" either. When Republican governor Wilson ran for reelection in the 1990s on a virulently anti-immigration platform, backing the infamous Proposition 187—which would have outlawed affirmative action, ended bilingual education, and denied drivers' licenses to undocumented workers—the campaign created such a significant backlash among California's Latino voters that they now vote overwhelmingly for Democrats.

The only Democrat to come close to Ann Richards's percentage of Hispanic voters in Texas was Tony Sanchez, the Democrats' "Dream Team" candidate for governor in 2002. Although there were no exit polls to verify his actual vote tally among Hispanics, some estimates put him winning close to 65 percent of the Hispanic vote in his losing race against Governor Rick Perry. That figure is probably a more realistic target for Democrats today. However, since the Sanchez effort, Hispanic votes for Democrats in statewide elections have been stuck on some sort of out-of-date, get-out-the-vote roller coaster that lurches along on the antiquated structure of the state Democratic Party. It's been a clunky climb up in one election and a steep drop in the next. The problem is more than mechanical.

Is Karl Rove Right?

Karl Rove has bragged that in Texas, "We get 40 percent of the Latino vote on average."[2] He's only slightly exaggerating. Too many Republicans have come close to that number to make Rove's statement a lie. Some recent surveys estimate that only about 27 percent of voting-age Hispanics actually identify themselves as Republicans.[3] So, if Republicans are winning as much as 40 percent of the Hispanic vote in recent elections, there are a lot of swing voters with Spanish surnames that Democrats are missing.

When Republicans really work the Hispanic vote with relevant messages, targeted mailings, and sophisticated media, they win Texas elections. That's exactly what George W. Bush did when he won reelection to the governor's office in 1998.

One reason Bush got 46 percent of the Hispanic vote was that his campaign carefully targeted Latino voters in El Paso, the border city that is the most heavily Democratic in the state, with its 82 percent Latino majority.

When as many as four out of every ten Hispanic voters are inclined to vote for Republicans under certain circumstances, Democrats can no longer swing a big GOTV net to drag Hispanics to the polls on Election Day. They have to be more selective and more discerning about what's happening among diverse Latino populations.

Nina Perales, vice president of the Mexican American Legal Defense and Education Fund, warns fellow Democrats that they have special problems with young Hispanics. "We're losing ground," she believes. "We have more U.S. citizen Latinos turning 18 every day than are getting registered. The gap between the eligible and the registered in the Latino community is widening, not narrowing."[4]

Texas's Hispanic population is young. Those who are under 17 represent about 37 percent of Texas's 10 million Hispanics. As these second- and third-generation youth move into the young adult years between 18 and 35, they are less engaged in the political world than their parents, now mostly in their 50s, 60s, or older. As James Aldrete, a Democratic consultant who specializes in Latino media has learned, "They are just not disposed to vote," he said. "Basically, we have to figure out how to politicize a nonpolitical group."[5]

Market research for businesses points to the complexities of selling products to today's Hispanic youth. Young Latinos live in a blended world of two cultures—the traditions and language of their parents and grandparents, and a totally Americanized experience of technology, music, social media, and mores. Marketers understand that there is not one monolithic Hispanic culture—but many. That's one more fact that most Texas Democrats have yet to consider. Who do Democrats need to reach to pump up their Hispanic support? Urbanized young people who are culturally hip? Young married couples who are just starting their families and shopping at Walmart? Upwardly mobile, college-educated professionals who are comfortable in the business world? Single men, a growing percentage of the Latino population, who may have dropped out of school and work menial jobs for minimum wage? Older families who cling to traditional values? And what about the new citizens from various Central American countries who now live here? That's a lot of groups, and each may require a different approach.

Although in Texas the vast majority of Latinos are Mexican American, there has been an influx of legal immigrants from other Spanish-speaking countries since 2000. By 2011, more than 3.1 million immigrants from Honduras, El Salvador, and Guatemala were living in the United States, and about 12 percent of these Central American newcomers are in Texas. Houston alone is home to more than 200,000.[6] The new immigrants have settled in other Texas cities as well. In some south San Antonio neighborhoods once dominated by working-class Mexican American families, the homes and schools are now filled with Salvadoran or Honduran families. The whole tone and tenor of life in those neighborhoods is different from what Democratic activists have encountered before in their traditional GOTV drives.

So what are Democrats going to do about all of these changes?

The answer is clear, but not easy.

Democrats simply have to work harder and smarter—and very differently from what they've always done. For starters, they have to pay closer attention to what Republicans are doing and why they have been so effective.

State representative Richard Peña Raymond, a 20-year veteran of Texas politics with experience in a variety of endeavors, is paying attention.

In 2014, he was alarmed when he noticed the positive impact on Latinos of a television ad featuring Republican gubernatorial candidate Greg Abbott's Mexican American mother-in-law. Here was a gentle grandmother who spoke with kindness about Abbott's values and his good heart, his love for family, God, and country. She sent a subtle signal to older Latino Catholics that they could trust Abbott because she had become his *madrina* (godmother and sponsor) when he joined the Catholic Church. The ad incorporated every soft, warm code word that marketers advise clients to use to sell products to older Hispanic buyers. The advertisement played in the Rio Grande Valley as well as in major markets like Dallas, Houston, and San Antonio with large Hispanic populations. When Raymond warned the Wendy Davis campaign that it needed a more intense focus on minority voters because Republicans were making headway with the ad, "They just brushed me off," he said.[7] After Abbott, with his sweet Mexican American mother-in-law, got 44 percent of the Hispanic vote in a notoriously low-turnout election, Raymond's optimism took a hit.

"I just don't know now," he said. "I used to think that our voters could have an impact by 2016 or 2018, but now I'm beginning to think it could be 2020 or 2022, or even beyond."

A six-term Democratic state rep from one of the most heavily Hispanic legislative districts in the nation, Raymond has been rooted in the South Texas brush country and most recently in the city of Laredo, the booming NAFTA gateway to the United States. Like many ambitious Hispanics who have wanted a future in Texas politics, Raymond got a law degree and worked for a couple of U.S. senators—first for the late Lloyd M. Bentsen in his home state of Texas and then for Paul Simon of Illinois. Raymond even ventured out of his safe South Texas district in 1998 to run for one of Texas's top five statewide offices, land commissioner. Although he was defeated in the landslide reelection of Governor George W. Bush over Garry Mauro, Raymond won a respectable 1.5 million votes.

Two years after the loss, Raymond returned to the legislature, took on various leadership roles, and devoted his political energies to helping other Democrats win local and statewide office—giving money, time, and energy to those Democrats bold enough to run for Texas governor against growing odds—millionaire banker Tony Sanchez in 2006 and former Houston mayor Bill White in 2010. Through it all, Raymond remained hopeful, and like most Democratic politicians in Texas, he continued to believe and recite the mantra, "Our day will come." For a time, he even thought that Wendy Davis might be the Democrat to break through. But after the 2014 miscues with Hispanic voters, he was beginning to grasp the reality that all Democrat leaders must face. They have to compete head-on with Republicans who know the only way to keep Texas perpetually red is to push their percentage of Latino support to over 40 percent in every election cycle.

Henry Cisneros, like Raymond, sees what might lie ahead if Democrats don't start paying attention to what's going on in Republican circles. Cisneros, once the great hope of Texas Democrats to be the first Mexican American governor or U.S. senator, was the first Latino mayor of San Antonio and went to Washington to serve in Bill Clinton's cabinet as secretary of housing and urban development. His promising political career came to an end when he got caught up in a scandal involving his former mistress.[8] Now older and far wiser, Cisneros is chair of CityView, a company that creates affordable housing in residential communities for middle-income families. His business has built over 60 communities in 13 states and provided housing to more than 7,000 people. In the midst of his business successes, Cisneros still worries about the future of his party and his state. He has told small gatherings of Democratic friends that if the party waits too long to figure out what's going on and delays too long in changing its approach, by the time Hispanics start voting in larger numbers, they'll be voting Republican.

Unlike the Democrats, however, Republicans are not simply waiting. They are trying a number of experiments to build a reliable bloc of Latino voters. In 2011, with $10 million in funding from Charles and David Koch's Freedom Partners and TC4 Trust, Republican operatives established the Libre Initiative, which they describe as a grassroots organization to "empower Hispanics" and advance "liberty, freedom and prosperity."[9] Libre Initiative set up offices in the Rio Grande Valley and has partner organizations in eight other states; its director is Daniel Garza, who once made an unsuccessful run for Congress as a Republican in the Rio Grande Valley. While Garza maintains that his organization is nonprofit and nonpartisan, he freely admits his association with the Koch brothers.

"I align with their values and what they're trying to do . . . I don't apologize for advancing the principles of economic freedom, of the free market, to try to advance more prosperity to the Latino community through the free market," he once said in a C-SPAN interview.[10] He also told a high school audience in Milwaukee that Libre's message "aligns more with Republicans because it's conservative and libertarian, and if Republicans benefit, so be it."[11] Libre has supported Texas's restrictive photo ID requirements for voting and has written op-ed pieces opposing minimum wage increases and the Affordable Care Act, all claiming that these measures actually harm Hispanics and limit their individual freedom. Fox News, which has heavily promoted Libre Initiative, has called the organization the "voice of the Hispanic community."[12]

While it seems like a stretch to convince Latino voters that having no health insurance or wage increases or being restricted in their right to vote actually gives them greater liberty, there is more going on within the group than position papers.

In the Rio Grande Valley, Libre Initiative holds regular citizenship training classes. Its staff identifies legal immigrants and offers free classes to help them prepare for the U.S. citizenship exam. Of course, the classes emphasize the free-market ideology at the heart of the Koch brothers' political activity. But Libre's instructors are also cultivating relationships with these new citizens in the hope that once they can vote, they will look with favor on those who helped them.

A second major effort to expand Libre's influence with Hispanics is to hold regional business summits, which are free for attendees. These programs, such as one held in Albuquerque in May 2015, offer opportunities for Latino business owners and professionals to mingle with Hispanic executives from major banks and businesses. While they have drawn small crowds, the seminars provide opportunities for ambitious Latino professionals (including those from nonprofit organizations) to establish networks with one another as well as those in the business world who share the same cultural heritage and experiences—all within the framework of Republican politics.

Efforts like these are long-term investments with two very different segments of the Latino population. Even so, many longtime Valley residents view the Koch operatives as slick, opportunistic outsiders, and it remains to be seen if they will be effective. However, Libre's work does show that Republicans are continuing to look for new ways to break Latino ties to the Democratic Party.

And, remember: Republicans don't have to win every Hispanic vote—only enough to get them above the magic 40 percent marker.

Republicans have also been making concerted efforts to recruit Latinos to run for office. While they've had some successes, they don't have much to brag about in the Texas legislature. When the 2015 legislative session got under way, there were no Latino Republicans in the state senate, and only five in the house of representatives, in contrast to 36 Hispanic Democrats. Yet one of their new legislators would like to become the first Hispanic governor of Texas. And he's telling anyone who will listen that he intends to be the voice of Hispanic Republicans.

The Hispanic Face of Republicanism

Forty-five-year-old Jason Villalba is a second-term Republican state representative from North Dallas. While Richard Raymond's South Texas legislative district is more than 90 percent Hispanic, Villalba's district is over 90 percent Anglo and considered as safe an election territory for Republicans as Raymond's district is for Democrats. Energetic, talkative, and oozing self-confidence, Villalba is determined to make his mark on Texas politics—and he exudes the kind of hope that Raymond is worried Democrats are losing. Villalba represents the potential breakthrough of young, professional Hispanics into the Republican Party in Texas.

As a little boy growing up in South Grand Prairie, a working-class area outside of Dallas, Villalba was taken with the optimism, rosy cheeks, and good nature of Ronald Reagan, whom he watched make a speech on TV during the 1980s. He decided then and there that he wanted to be a Republican. "I'm not a recovering

Democrat," he said. "I never was a Democrat . . . I found Jesus at a church summer camp when I was about seven, and then the next year I found Ronald Reagan, both of whom had equal influences on my life in a lot of ways."[13]

Attorney Villalba is the kind of Hispanic who gives the Republicans hope—professional, affluent, and part of a growing segment of ambitious young men and women who seek power and influence and believe they have a better opportunity to find it within the Texas GOP. Although a strong adherent of standard Republican orthodoxy, Villalba has made it quite clear that he is not part of the extreme right wing of his party. "I represent my neighbors, not the Tea Party," he says. "I'm a common-sense Republican. I represent the people who live in the middle. I am like them. So ordinary that we're extraordinary."[14]

Villalba's Dallas district is anything but ordinary. It includes some of Dallas's most exclusive and expensive neighborhoods, including multimillion-dollar homes in Preston Hollow, and the separate municipalities of Highland Park and University Park, where billionaires like Dallas Cowboys owner Jerry Jones and Ross Perot live. Only about 5 percent of its residents are Hispanic, and during his first campaign over 60 percent of those Hispanics voted for his Anglo Democratic opponent.

Villalba's upbringing provides clues about how he became a Republican rather than a Democrat. His Mexican American parents both had difficult childhoods and essentially grew up on their own without much help from family or friends. Neither was able to graduate from high school, and they married when they were only 17, while she was a checkout clerk at a grocery store and he was a bagger. They lived their entire lives in the same small home, and only later in life did they each manage to get a GED. "To them, education was the most important thing for me and my sister," Villalba remembered. "They saw to it that we studied and worked hard. We were taught to be self-reliant. My parents learned at a young age that they had to be self-reliant and that's what they taught us. It's probably one of the reasons I'm a Republican—self-reliance is in the DNA of all Republicans."

Villalba's hard work won him a scholarship to Baylor University and a law degree from the University of Texas at Austin. He landed a job with one of Dallas's premier corporate law firms where he found his professional niche handling mergers and acquisitions. His business associates reinforced his conservative beliefs, particularly the conviction that most government social service programs create dependence rather than self-reliance.

That belief in self-reliance became the foundation for just about everything else Villalba believes. That's why he's against Social Security and Medicaid and other programs that he believes promote dependency rather than self-sufficiency.

"The Democrats trade favors for votes. They create programs that feed a constituency that in turn rewards them with votes," he says. Long-term financial implications of these programs worry him as well. "That's why Republicans are against Obamacare—it's just another government giveaway program without worry about the cost."

While his family upbringing and association with wealthy clients help account for his conservative philosophy, there is one more clue that even Villalba does not seem to recognize as a stepping stone to his Republican affiliation. Villalba was raised in a Bible church—"not exactly fundamentalist," he says, but an old-fashioned church where the Bible was preached, praised, taught, and memorized. Villalba's wife was raised Catholic, and shortly after they married they shopped around for a church they could attend as a family. They became Methodists, where there was less focus on sin than Villalba's Bible church and fewer rituals than his wife's Catholic church.

The Protestant Villalba family, which now includes two children, represents part of a growing trend among Hispanics, who are leaving the Catholic Church for a variety of reasons—some spiritual, with a longing for a more experiential religious connection; some for the desire to belong to a more vibrant and personal community; and some, perhaps, for social advancement and upward mobility. Although the Catholic Church is still the largest denomination in the United States, its share of Latinos has dropped from 67 percent to 55 percent since 2010.[15] While it is of special concern to the bishops and the entire Catholic hierarchy, why does this matter in the political world?

Non-Catholic Hispanics who are born-again or evangelical Christians have become a major target for Republican recruitment. And today, about one in four Latinos is Protestant, including 16 percent who describe themselves as evangelical. The new evangelical and fundamentalist Latinos are generally conservative not only in their religious beliefs, but also in their worldview. They tend to be much more conservative than their Catholic counterparts on both social and economic issues. More than two-thirds oppose gay marriage, and most believe that churches should be more involved in conservative political and social issues. According to a Pew Research Center report on religious identity of Hispanics, more than 30 percent of all evangelical Hispanics identify themselves as Republicans.[16]

The evangelical churches, with their strong foothold within the Republican Party, reach out to Hispanics who are moving up the economic ladder. They also provide a social safety net when Hispanic families lose jobs or face health issues or other problems. The churches help with basic needs like food, clothing, and health care. Many of the larger churches maintain health clinics or food pantries in a more direct form of service than traditional Catholic charities.

While this significant social change is still relatively recent, it has caught the eye of Republican operatives. And it may account for one of the reasons that Texas Hispanics are giving Republicans close to 40 percent of their votes in some elections.

Jason Villalba wants to be their leader, as well as the voice of all family-oriented Latinos. "I want to be an example of opportunity for young people," he said. He is open about his ambition and thinks that he has what it takes to be the first Hispanic governor of Texas. He uses the word "opportunity" a lot in his conversations and speeches. He believes the opportunity under the Republican banner for someone with his upbringing is something that can inspire other Hispanics to follow his lead.

Just like the old days in the Democratic Party, when ambitious personalities clashed and factions fought for ascendency, there is at least one other Republican who stands in his way.

We Just Can't Get Rid of the Bushes

Just when we thought we'd had enough, here comes another Bush. This time it is 40-year old George P. Bush, son of Jeb, nephew of George W., and grandson of George H. W. George P. is half

Mexican, dashingly good-looking, and by 2014 had already been elected to statewide office.

His first public act as land commissioner, the officer who takes cares of Texas's vast public lands, was somewhat puzzling. He decided to take away the management of the sacred Alamo from the little old Anglo ladies who saved it from destruction at the beginning of the twentieth century and have been running it ever since. It's true that the Daughters of the Republic of Texas had let it deteriorate a bit and had not exactly been careful financial stewards of the state's most famous tourist site. But to throw the Daughters of the Republic of Texas out of the 300-year-old mission—well, that's a little too much, even for a Bush. After all, the Alamo is at the center of Texas's almost mythical beginning, the site of the historic last stand of Davy Crockett, James Bowie, and 150 martyred Texans who died fighting for independence in the 13-day siege by the Mexican army led by General Antonio López de Santa Anna. A Hispanic Republican who runs for higher office is still going to have to win over Anglo voters. Attacking the little old ladies who are the modern-day defenders of Texas's most important shrine may not be the best way to do it. Still, the old Bush money crowd hovers and will no doubt come around when the new Bush needs it to run for higher office.

Texas, however, is not his for the taking just yet. Some Republicans like Jason Villalba don't much like this Floridian coming into their state and trying to claim it as his own. Although "P," as some call him, was born in Houston, earned a law degree from the University of Texas, and has in recent years practiced law in Fort Worth, he spent most of his life in Florida. That rubs some ambitious Latino politicians the wrong way—Democrats and Republicans.

"Well, he's smart and a good friend of mine," Jason Villalba says. "But he really doesn't come from the same background that I do. I come from the poor. We were poor people, and like most Mexicans in Texas, we were not born with silver spoons in our mouths. We came up with nothing; we had to scratch our way up. That's not what Bush had to do. And besides, he has the burden of carrying the name 'Bush.'"

The gentle chiding carried over into the race for the Republican nomination for the 2016 presidential election. Villalba picked Marco Rubio over Jeb Bush because "he embodies the Republican spirit of opportunity. He relates better to how I grew up . . . he's not the son of a congressman or governor or president. He came up the hard way, like I did."

While Democrats might enjoy watching this kind of rivalry develop and one day turn into a major primary fight for higher office among Hispanic Republicans, that kind of scenario is fraught with peril. An expensive, hard-fought Republican primary battle between two attractive Mexican American candidates has the potential to draw thousands of new Latino voters into their primary to vote. Once in, it will become even harder for Democrats to entice them back out.

So . . . is it all doom and gloom for the Democrats?

No. Not at all.

There are any number of Latino Democrats who are as smart as they are ambitions, and many of them already hold public office. Congressman Pete Gallego, of southwestern Texas, thinks strategically, knows the ropes, and has represented one of the nation's few swing congressional districts—where Democrats win in presidential election years when the voter turnout is high, and lose in off years when the turnout is lower. Dallas's Rafael Anchia has become a strong leader in the Texas legislature, as have Trey Martinez Fischer, from San Antonio; Celia Israel, from Austin; and state senator Sylvia R. Garcia, from Houston. There are other emerging leaders from all over the state. Hispanic Democrats continue to draw a higher percentage of Latino voters when they are on the ballot than just about any Latino Republican—even one who hopes to be the new face of Hispanic power in Texas.

The Mother of Hope:
Rosie Castro and Her Boys

No conversation about hope that the Hispanic vote will turn Texas blue is complete without some mention of the 42-year-old twin Castro brothers—Joaquin and Julián. Joaquin serves in the U.S. House of Representatives from San Antonio, and Julián, the former mayor of San Antonio, serves in President Obama's cabinet as secretary of housing and urban development. He is often mentioned as a possible vice presidential nominee in 2016. Could the twin brothers represent the future for Democrats in Texas?

Their mother, Maria del Rosario Castro—Rosie—was a dynamic community activist and organizer for La Raza Unida during the height of the Chicano third-party movement in the 1970s. The Castro brothers were steeped in the political radicalism of their mother, but they have emerged as cautious Democratic Party centrists. Although the brothers are not yet well known in all parts of Texas, many hope that at least one of the brothers will run for statewide office. But questions abound. Can they inspire non-voting Hispanics to vote? Can they pull sufficient numbers of white swing voters to make a difference? Can they raise the money it will take to win? Will they risk their rising careers on an "iffy" race for state office? And if one or the other decides to enter state-wide politics, what might be the optimal time to take the plunge?

As I look back on my years in Texas politics, which actually began in San Antonio in the 1960s, I see a history of Texas Mexican American activism culminating in the lives of these two impressive young men. I remember their mother, Rosie Castro, well. She was a student at the all-Catholic girls college Our Lady of the Lake, where she organized a chapter of the Young Democrats. That is where she learned to canvass door-to-door and distribute bumper stickers for candidates. She joked that she and her friends became known as the "bumper-sticker queens."[17]

Smart, passionate, and articulate, Rosie Castro was unbelievably outspoken for a young Mexican American woman at the time. I used to see her at weekly political luncheons at Karam's Mexican restaurant on San Antonio's West Side. I was a young wife and mother getting my first introduction to hardball politics. Rosie represented the new minority youth movement within the Democratic Party. I think we both felt privileged to sit at the feet of the Mexican American icons of the era—state senator Joe Bernal, city councilman Pete Torres, state representative Johnny Alaniz. We were particularly fortunate to rub shoulders with civil rights leader G. J. Sutton, who would become the first African American from San Antonio to serve in the Texas legislature. Master political strategist Herschel Bernard put together the money for the progressive coalition and had a wry sense of humor that could bring tedious discussions to a swift end.[18] The meetings always took on additional gravitas when Bexar County Commissioner Albert Peña attended.

Peña had headed the Viva Kennedy organization during the 1960 presidential election, and he was the most significant mentor for an awakening generation of Latinos who were getting their first taste of political power. My late husband, John Rogers, while serving as the president of the local chapter of the American Newspaper Guild, which had organized editorial workers at the now-defunct *San Antonio Light*, started writing speeches for Peña, and we both actively supported the new Hispanic activism that we believed provided hope for the transformation of San Antonio's conservative all-Anglo political structure. John's antiestablishment views got him tagged "El Extremo," and by default I was "Mrs. Extremo," which probably got me into those weekly meetings of San Antonio's new coalition of progressive activists—East Side blacks, West Side Mexican Americans, North Side white liberals, plus a half-dozen local union leaders and a few college professors from St. Mary's University. There was a lot of big talk at those luncheons, and sometimes actual political strategies emerged.

"It was heady stuff. It was an incredible learning experience for me," Rosie Castro remembered.[19] And I felt the same way watching the give and take in serious political discussions and learning how older, wiser people worked out their differences.

In the late 1960s, as a more militant, youthful Chicano movement spread from Los Angeles to San Antonio, young Rosie Castro got tired of waiting for slow evolutionary change to come out of those meetings. As a fierce and formidable advocate for Chicanos, she became part of the more radical, youth-oriented La Raza Unida political party, which in 1970 elected the mayor and took over the city government in Crystal City, just south of San Antonio. Yet Castro stayed close to her roots in San Antonio, where she had grown up, sometimes going with her single mother to clean the houses of wealthy Anglos on the North Side. Castro ran twice, unsuccessfully, for a seat on the San Antonio City Council. When her sons were born in 1974, they barely slowed her down. Her mother helped raise the twins after Rosie and their father, public school teacher Jesse Guzman, separated when the boys were eight. Still, they often tagged along with their mother to rallies and protests. Julián once wrote in a college essay that political slogans "rang in my ears like war cries. '*Viva La Raza!*,' 'Black and Brown United!'"[20] But the Castro brothers grew up in a very different era from their mother.

The kind of evolutionary change that tested Rosie Castro's patience had actually taken place over time in San Antonio. By 1981 Henry Cisneros had become the city's first Hispanic mayor. Mexican Americans made up a majority of the city's legislative delegation in Austin, and the community-organizing efforts of a MacArthur Foundation "genius grant" fellow, Ernesto Cortes, had created one of the most powerful minority community coalitions in the nation, Communities Organized for Public Service (COPS). Beginning in the 1970s, the group taught church leaders and PTA moms how to use political power to bring change to San Antonio's poorest neighborhoods, forcing the city to initiate floodwater controls and sewer improvements on the largely Hispanic West Side. Later, COPS members became major players in

Texas public-school reform efforts in the 1980s. In this different atmosphere Rosie Castro's boys thrived. They excelled in public schools and had the benefit of a Stanford undergraduate education as well as law degrees from Harvard. All that Rosie Castro had worked for had come to fruition—perhaps not in the way she had originally envisioned, but in a way that enabled her more centrist sons to succeed beyond her wildest dreams.

In 2001, Julián was elected to the San Antonio city council 30 years after his mother had sought the same job. Later, he became a three-term mayor of San Antonio. His signature accomplishment was a huge, citywide expansion of a pre-kindergarten education program called Pre-K for SA. Because he had spent years cultivating the city's business leaders, he was able to count on their support for the program, which San Antonio voters overwhelmingly approved in a bond issue. With his mother watching from the gallery, he gave a ringing Democratic National Convention keynote address in 2012—following in the footsteps of two other notable Texans who electrified earlier conventions: Barbara Jordan in 1976 and Ann Richards in 1988. President Obama later tapped him for a cabinet post, where he continues to draw national attention, and possibly a vice-presidential nomination in the future.

With national attention focused on Julián, it is Joaquin who political insiders think about when considering which of the Castro brothers might make a mark at home. His experience in state politics and policy is deeper than his brother's. Joaquin served five terms in the Texas House of Representatives before running for Congress in 2013 and taking over the 20th congressional district, which had been occupied by the incomparable, often mercurial, Henry B. Gonzalez for 38 years, followed by his son, Charlie.

Henry Gonzalez's framed photo is still on the walls in the homes of many of San Antonio's older Mexican American families because he was their first champion, the one who knew their aspirations and deepest hopes. Joaquin is well aware of that legacy and of the obligation to carry on the tradition.

Since the 2014 Democratic electoral wipeout, Joaquin has talked privately with key donors and some of the wise old sages of the Democratic Party about what might be done to jump-start some sort of Democratic resurgence. And he has some ideas himself, particularly about how key issues could be developed to point out to voters what Republican cuts to social services actually mean in the daily lives of ordinary people.

When Republicans slashed state funding for nursing homes, Joaquin felt it was a perfect issue to use with voters. "You could run that on the radio all day," he told reporter Andy Kroll. "You need to sear it in people's brains so the next time they go, 'Hey, I remember—these are the guys who wanted to cut your nursing-home funding.'"[21] Joaquin Castro is obviously trying to figure out how to break through Democratic and Hispanic apathy. "We've got to develop a political infrastructure that can operate between elections," he said. "It would involve [a] year-round coordinated media and message operation to rebuild the Democratic Party image with Texas voters."[22]

"I'm always thinking about politics," he once told a reporter. "What is going on here? What is missing here? We still haven't figured out the formula in Texas."[23]

It is clear that Joaquin Castro wants to be part of that formula, whatever it turns out to be. And the donors and business leaders who still lean Democratic obviously hope he will be part of it, one way or another. One prominent business leader told me that he found the congressman serious and thoughtful about all aspects of policies and politics, and impressive in his realistic assessment of what's happening among Democrats today.

Like Republican Jason Villalba, Joaquin Castro also talks about opportunity for Hispanics in Texas. But his understanding of the conditions that actually provide opportunity run much deeper. In a long article about his first year in Congress for *Texas Monthly* magazine in early 2014, Castro wrote of the need to create an "infrastructure of opportunity." The essay was unusually introspective and revealing of who he is and what he wants:

> What would it be like if I didn't care, if I hadn't grown up going to marches and campaign rallies since the age of three, if I hadn't lain awake at night and listened to my parents talking about the injustice of the schools in our part of town getting less money? I was not programmed to go into politics. I was taught to care. I still believe that government matters in people's lives, not when it's big or small but when it's purposeful. It can help build what I think of as the infrastructure of opportunity.[24]

To Joaquin Castro, that infrastructure has to include good schools, well-paying jobs, health care, safe neighborhoods, and the basics that allow people to live productive lives.

"We've got a basic conflict about this," he says. "There are people who want to build up that kind of infrastructure and there are those who want to tear it down. As Democrats, we haven't yet been able to get that across."

Whether Joaquin Castro decides to stay in the U.S. Congress or run for attorney general, governor, or senator, or simply help Democrats figure out what they can do to create that "infrastructure of opportunity," his voice is one that will be considered among those who are seriously trying to figure out how to turn Texas blue. It may be too soon for him to undertake a statewide race, and his future in politics is still linked personally and politically to what his twin brother Julián decides to do.

The symbiosis between the brothers could be either a help or a hindrance. Political consultant Christian Archer, who has managed campaigns for both brothers, observed that "any mistake on Joaquin's campaign, and you are messing with Julián." It goes the other way, too. In Julián's campaign, Archer remembered, "Joaquin could be aggressive as well," demanding e-mail statistics and fund-raising reports.[25] If each gets so consumed with his own political career, that kind of watchful oversight for one another might be more difficult to manage. But elective office may not be the only option on the table.

Joaquin says, "I've been around politics since I was three years old. There are lots of other things I would like to pursue."

Whatever they ultimately decide, both of the Castro brothers present some interesting options for Texas Democrats, and they bear watching.

NINE

A New Texas Way

THIS IS WHAT SCARES TEXAS REPUBLICANS:

- They know they have reached their peak white vote.
- They can't get much higher than the 90 percent they now draw in some rural areas or small Texas towns.
- Their percentage of white voters in urban areas is declining, and although they won't admit it publicly, it will begin to do so in the suburbs as well.
- They have no room to expand in Texas's African American communities, which provide the most consistently loyal support to Democrats of any segment of the population.
- They are beginning to lose younger, more liberal Asian voters, even though their parents may generally vote Republican.
- If Democrats can prevent Republicans in statewide races from getting more than 35 percent of the Hispanic vote,

Republicans are going to be in serious trouble as they approach 2018.

There are three main factors that give Democrats reason to believe that Republicans could lose political power in Texas.

First, the Republicans' hard-line approach to immigration and border security alienates most Latinos. Second, their intraparty personal rivalries and internal conflicts over the increasing craziness and wacko legislation that pops out of the Texas legislature have already begun to tear them apart. And third, the diversity explosion in solidly Republican suburbs has the potential to dilute the most reliable segment of their base.[1]

Finally, there are some actions that Democrats have been smart enough to take on local levels since 2006 that could further increase the party's base in the cities.

For now, Democrats might be getting a little help from distant places.

The Pope Effect

Is Pope Francis a secret liberal? That's what Republicans fear and Texas Democrats might hope.

Nationally, Republicans are worried about how influential the Pope might be with his messages of conciliation, tolerance for gays and divorced Catholics, plus his renewed emphasis on the social justice teachings of the Church, which just do not mesh well with the extreme free-market Republican ideology. Especially troubling for GOP candidates is the Pope's encyclical on climate change. The document established a moral standard for dealing with the reality of global warming and boosted scientific claims that human activity is a causal factor in increasing environmental disasters.[2] Because the poor are most seriously affected by extreme weather changes, the Pope's message was a call to action. Republican politicians fear that this Pope is more than just a religious leader. He might be a political leader as well.[3] It's not often that prominent Republicans take potshots at the Pope, but their grumblings aren't secret.

"This guy is from Argentina . . . they haven't had real capitalism," complained Congressman (and former GOP vice presidential candidate) Paul W. Ryan. Jeb Bush didn't like the Pope's role in opening the doors for the United States's diplomatic breakthrough with Cuba. Marco Rubio just wishes that the Pope would "take up the cause of freedom and democracy."[4] These guys ought to be worried, considering what happened to the GOP in 2012. Obama won the nation's Catholic vote by 52 to 48 percent, and Hispanic Catholics gave Obama 76 percent of their votes. Catholics still make up the largest religious denomination in the country, and Republicans can't afford to lose many more of their votes.

"When you talk about Catholics, there are really two Catholic votes, the white vote and the Hispanic vote, which look starkly different," says Robert Jones, chief executive of the Public Religion Research Institute.[5] Exit polls in 2012 showed that most Latino voters were focused on economic issues, not on Catholic positions on abortion or gay marriage.

Republicans worry about this trend and the fact that Pope Francis is providing wiggle room for some of his American bishops to shift focus away from abortion issues to emphasize the Church's social justice message.

Josephine Lopez Paul, a former schoolteacher from New Mexico who is now the lead community organizer for Dallas Area Interfaith, believes the new Pope is making the Church relevant again by focusing more on issues that matter in the everyday lives of parishioners. "While they may be pro-life, young Catholics don't necessarily want abortion to be the only issue front and center for the Church," she says.[6]

Paul, along with other Hispanic leaders, emphasized the importance of Pope Francis's recent document, "The Joy of the Gospel," which has become an important teaching tool for the Church. The Pope called for a "church which is for the poor . . . we are called to lend our voices to their causes, but also to be their friends, to listen to them, to speak for them and to embrace them." Preached in Sunday homilies, study groups, Catholic schools, and laity conferences, the document teaches that charity is more than mere handouts: "It means working to eliminate the structural causes of poverty and to promote the integral development of the poor." For the Pope and the new direction of the Church under his leadership, this means that education, access to health care, and employment are central to the development and dignity of the poor.[7]

Jacob Cortes, like Josephine Paul, is a community organizer. He works with Austin Interfaith, part of the Southwest Industrial Areas Foundation (IAF) Network, as is Dallas Interfaith.[8] With activities centered in Catholic parishes, Protestant churches, and Jewish synagogues, Cortes teaches community leaders how to advocate for the needs of working families. The Dallas and Austin Interfaith groups grew out of the COPS experience in San Antonio, and organizers like Cortes and Paul are acutely aware of the everyday concerns of people most often neglected by big-time politicians. Jacob Cortes believes that Pope Francis's emphasis on working with the poor has the potential to spark the idealism of young Catholics and motivate them to get involved in their communities. "Priests are now telling parishioners that they have to connect with the poor," he says, and he believes that idealistic youth in those parishes are closely following the pronouncements of Pope Francis.[9]

In the 1960s, after Pope John XXIII convened the Second Vatican Council to bring the Church into the modern age, Catholics—and particularly the younger generations—were inspired to get involved in community action programs as well as in political endeavors. It was one of the transformational moments that awakened many in Latino communities to the need for political involvement to solve issues of discrimination and persistent poverty. If Pope Francis's words and deeds begin to inspire that kind of activism, then a significant portion of the burgeoning Hispanic youth culture might be more motivated to register and vote in Texas elections. For now, Hispanic youth, along with their parents, are engaged primarily in only one major public issue: immigration reform. And Republicans are finding themselves on the wrong side of that issue across the board.

The Dreamers

During the marathon debates of the 2012 Republican presidential primaries, Governor Rick Perry shocked his party's right-wing base by bragging about his Texas version of the Dream Act, which allowed undocumented college students who had lived in Texas for at least three years to pay the in-state tuition rate at Texas's colleges and universities. In 2001, Texas was the first state in the union to open its college doors to undocumented young immigrants at the lower rates, and since then about 16,000 students a year have taken advantage of the program.[10] Although Perry quickly dropped the issue before his "oops" moment derailed his campaign, it's true that he and moderate Republicans in Texas had largely shied away from punishing the children of undocumented Latino immigrants. But that began to change by 2012 when Texas Tea Party Republicans embraced an anti-immigration xenophobia long before celebrity GOP presidential candidate Donald Trump made it the centerpiece of his campaign.

In 2015, the rallying cry of Texas governor Greg Abbott and his ideological doppelganger, Lieutenant Governor Dan Patrick, was "border security." In a grand political gesture, they spent more than $800 million to buy more surveillance equipment and send more state troopers to the border to "help" the federal government do its job. Federal officials on the ground never asked for the help and complained (off the record) that the state's obsession with border security often complicated their operations. Although immigrants from Mexico make up more than half of those who come here without papers, illegal crossings from Mexico have consistently declined over the past few years, dropping by almost a million since 2007. What's more, the surge of women and children from Central America in 2014 has virtually ended.[11] Yet Texas officials persist in their racially tinged rhetoric about border security because it stirs up their right-wing base of voters as few other issues do.

Republican congressman Louie Gohmert of East Texas, who can always be counted on to say something outrageous and often untrue, reflects the tone too often used by public officials here. He claimed that President Obama's immigration policies were "luring millions of diseased immigrant children" to the United States.[12] And he urged Texas officials to "'use whatever means' possible, like troops, ships of war, or taxes to 'stop the invasion.'"[13]

Although few Democrats pay much attention to Gohmert, they worried that Lieutenant Governor Dan Patrick, a former radio talk show host from Houston, might inflict real damage. With his legislative policy advisory committee composed mostly of Tea Party activists, Patrick was determined to implement the state Republican Party's platform calling for repeal of the Dream Act and the prohibition of "sanctuary" cities, which offer assistance to undocumented immigrants in need of help. Patrick echoed Gohmert and claimed that the surge of immigrant mothers and children who crossed the Texas border during the summer of 2014 were bringing third-world diseases into the state—tuberculosis, malaria, polio, and leprosy—all decidedly untrue, according to Texas public health officials. "Stop the invasion" has been his battle cry. "We are being overrun. It is imperiling our safety."[14]

The fear of hordes of Latino immigrants taking over neighborhoods and communities certainly has elements of pure racism at its core. And that's what young Texas Hispanics pick up on. The efforts in 2015 to repeal the Texas Dream Act energized them, and students organized rallies on college campuses, staged protests at the state Capitol, testified before legislative committees, and enlisted powerful people across the state to help. The chancellor of the vast University of Texas system, with its 200,000 students on nine campuses and at six medical schools, came out against repealing the measure. The proposed legislation stalled and finally died after Texas business leaders also weighed in against repeal.

"If Texas goes the wrong way on this issue, these Dreamers will be virtually denied an education, and that would not be good for Texas," said Bill Hammond, president of the Texas Association of Business.[15]

Latino legislators gave full credit, however, to the students who fought the anti-immigrant bills. State representative Rafael Anchia of Dallas praised the advocacy groups and the young immigrants. "We did our work on the inside game," he said, "but the outside game was dominated really by the Dreamers."[16]

Jason Villalba worries that his party could lose a whole generation of Mexican American voters if it lets the hard right continue to focus on repealing the Texas Dream Act. "If we lose the hearts and minds, we'll be in trouble. All of us know someone who is undocumented . . . a *tia* or *tio*, an *abuelita*. We can't shut them out. It's personal."

Tea Party leaders were not at all happy when the Dream Act survived. Ridding Texas of immigrants is still a key issue for almost 60 percent of Republicans in Texas. Research after the 2014 midterm elections showed that 75 percent of voters who believed that illegal immigrants should be summarily deported voted for Republican candidates.[17]

Tea Party members heaped scorn on Republican legislators who didn't swallow the whole anti-immigrant agenda, not to mention their failure to enact the myriad anti-gay issues laid out in the Republican Party platform.

"We wanted the Legislature to remove the magnets (for illegal immigration) and make a strong push for enforcement," Tea Party leader Katrina Pierson complained. Reverend Dave Welch of the Texas Pastor Council Action network added, "It is an astounding and appalling reality that in one of the most Republican-dominated state governments in the U.S., that the Texas legislature did nothing meaningful to protect religious freedom, traditional marriage or oppose the radical agenda of sexual gender confusion."[18]

Internal conflicts linger because the Tea Party didn't win every item on its radical agenda. The resulting turmoil might allow a few savvy Democrats to build new bridges to long-neglected moderate corporate executives. Hostility toward immigrants and angry rhetoric about same-sex marriage is simply bad for business.

Plague of Internal Conflicts

If you're in power, you can't escape the internal turmoil, competing factions, corruption charges, and personal ambitions that begin to pull your party apart. Republicans are now facing what Democrats had to deal with throughout the twentieth century. And it's not only about the Texas Dream Act or illegal border crossings.

When Tea Party favorite Texas attorney general Ken Paxton was indicted on three felony counts of securities fraud violations during the summer of 2015, Republican officials were noticeably silent, obviously fearful about getting embroiled in a sensational blowback related to the state's top legal eagle facing criminal charges.[19] But that's not the only problem facing the new reactionary group of officeholders.

During the 2015 legislative session, rumors flooded Capitol hallways about tensions between the top three Republican officeholders—governor, lieutenant governor, and Speaker of the house. The disputes spilled over into public view after it became apparent that some legislation passed by the right-wing senate was failing to come up for consideration in the house of representatives. Emboldened by his victory over the failed Tea Party challenge to his leadership, House Speaker Joe Straus blocked several senate bills with the obvious hope of killing them. A particularly bitter clash played out for weeks in the news media over who would get almost $4 billion in tax cuts that both the house and senate supported. As expected, Texas's businesses got the bulk of the cuts—almost $2.5 billion—but the leader of each chamber wanted something in the bill that would look good to ordinary Texans. House members wanted a sales tax cut that might benefit everyone, but the senate wanted a property tax cut that would help homeowners. The senate got its way and Texas raised its homestead exemption by $10,000, effectively giving homeowners about $125 a year off their tax bill—hardly worth the effort.

The increasingly irrelevant governor, Greg Abbott, did his best to avoid taking a position on the dueling tax bills, obviously not wanting to offend either the Tea Party or Republican business leaders. Insiders reported that in regularly scheduled weekly meetings with the lieutenant governor and the Speaker, Governor Abbott rarely said a word. When asked what he thought about this or that bill coming up for consideration, Abbott demurred, hedged, and refused to say anything until he knew what Dan Patrick was planning to do. Abbott was obviously worried that Patrick, with his vast Tea Party support, would challenge him when up for re-election in 2018. And that may well be the case. In Texas politics, ambition rules and power wins. And within the Texas Republican Party, Dan Patrick has the power for now.

In the spring of 2015, Abbott made an amazingly bizarre move to bolster his standing with the Tea Party. U.S. military training maneuvers were scheduled across seven states, including Texas. The exercises involved elite special operations forces, such as the Navy SEALS and the Green Berets, and included 1,200 personnel. Online chatter among right-wing groups, fueled by radio host and conspiracy theorist Alex Jones, warned that U.S. military forces were planning to take over the states and declare martial law, plus take away the guns of law-abiding citizens. Governor Abbott bought into the craziness and ordered the Texas State Guard to monitor the military exercises to make sure the state would not be taken over by federal troops![20] Except for one lone Republican, the action drew little initial skepticism or concern from other GOP leaders. Former state representative Todd Smith accused the governor of "pandering to idiots" and released a letter branding Abbott's action as "embarrassing." He wondered whether Abbott "actually believes this stuff " or simply "doesn't have the backbone to stand up to those who do." Smith practically begged for like-minded rational Republicans to speak up. "Is there *anybody* who is going to stand up to this radical nonsense that is a cancer on our state and our party?"[21]

After being ridiculed mercilessly in the national press, only a few Republicans were shamed into speaking up about this "nonsense." They simply didn't want to get too far ahead of their Tea Party supporters. Rick Perry said it was okay to attack the government, but perhaps Abbott was taking it a little too far by attacking the military!

Trouble is, that kind of "radical nonsense" still plays well in Republican primary elections. It's going to be hard for anyone to get further out on the extremist fringe than Dan Patrick, but Greg Abbott is certainly giving it a try. When the legislature ended its

2015 session, top leaders made nice with each other publicly. Don't expect the tension to diminish, however. It will just play out behind the scenes until it pops out again during the next election cycle.

At the end of 2015, other GOP rivalries and conflicts emerged at lower levels. Will Jason Villalba or George P. Bush prove to be *numero uno* among Hispanic Republicans? Will the hard-liners or the pragmatists set the tone for future discussions about immigration, border security, taxes, and social policy? Will Michael Quinn Sullivan, the Tea Party "enforcer," set such ridiculous standards of pure orthodoxy that officeholders rebel against his influence? Will the Koch brothers' money have any impact at all?

None of that may matter if Democrats take advantage of the shifts under way in suburbia and develop a swing-voter strategy that captures new Hispanic voters as well as disaffected Anglo Republicans. The opportunities exist in places Democrats rarely visit during election season.

The New Suburbia

In the 1980s, Texas suburbs were drawing Rust Belt job-seekers who voted Republican. They helped turn Texas into a solid red state.

A different kind of movement to the suburbs is under way today. For the first time since the Great Migration in the early days of the twentieth century, when more than 5 million African Americans left the South for the North and West, the process is being reversed. African Americans, mostly middle-class professionals, are moving back to the South, and most are settling in suburban communities. Houston and Dallas, along with Atlanta and Washington, D.C., experienced the largest increases in their black populations from 2000 to 2010 because of this new migration.[22] Now more than of half of African Americans who live in metropolitan areas are in the suburbs.

And why not? Since the 1970s, this is where families with children have gone to find good schools, parks, lower crime rates, and bigger houses for less money than within the cities.

Hispanics and Asians are also following the old path of white flight to the suburbs. "They are all aspiring to achieve the American Dream," writes demographer William Frey.[23] About half of the nation's suburban population gain since 2000 is attributable to Hispanics, both native-born and immigrant.[24] "The rise of new minority populations, the sharp slowdown of white population growth, and the economic gains and increased residential freedom of new generations . . . are rapidly changing the classic image of suburbanization," according to Frey. Together the trends paint a picture of population dynamics in cities and suburbs that is vastly different from what Texas candidates and political consultants, as well as the public, considers typical. The 2010 census showed that the majority of each of the nation's largest racial minority groups now resides in the suburbs.[25]

Texas suburbs and cities are attracting new white residents too. Contrary to the political leanings of those who flocked to Texas in the 1970s and 1980s, these migrants may lean blue. Many are from California, and they have a habit of voting Democratic. In 2010, after the Manhattan Institute for Policy Research, a conservative think tank founded in 1978 by William J. Casey (who later became President Ronald Reagan's CIA director), published research showing that Texas is the number-one destination for members of

California's middle-class white population who decide to leave their state, right-wing bloggers started fretting about the future of Texas politics.[26] The worry is that these new residents will strengthen the Democratic Party's potential in Texas and weaken the GOP's grip. Texas cities, and in particular their suburbs, are attracting migrants from other blue states as well. Chalk it up to a warmer climate, lack of a state income tax, new job opportunities, or lower housing costs. The fact is that many of the new migrants coming to Texas from other parts of the country seem quite willing to vote for Democrats.

In Texas, Austin is a destination for the young, affluent, and liberal, and like Raleigh, Denver, and Atlanta, its white population is growing. Austin was the only city in Texas that actually produced an *increase* in turnout among Democrats in the disastrous 2014 Democratic loss. According to exit polling, the higher turnout was attributed to an increase in the number of progressive white voters.

Dallas and Houston are moving in that direction. Both have large and vibrant gay communities that have brought new diversity to those cities. Houston elected openly gay Annise Parker to serve as mayor for three terms. The renewed local and national focus on progressive sociocultural issues in these metropolitan areas holds appeal for younger voters, professionals, gays, and women. These voters are more socially tolerant and don't seem to fear the progressive actions of "big government." *National Journal* writer Ronald Brownstein has called these groups the "coalition of the ascendant" and predicts that Democrats could pick up support from white college graduates, particularly among the millennial generation.[27]

If Texas Democrats want to expand their base vote and increase voter turnout in future elections, plus slice margins off Republican votes in the suburbs, they might start by taking the fight to

Republican turf. The number of Democratic voters in the suburbs is increasing in presidential elections, although they have not yet materialized in off-year state elections. For example, in the key suburban Republican area of Fort Bend County outside Houston, the minority population has increased by 97 percent since 2000, and Democratic voting strength has improved by 8 percent. Even in conservative Brazos County, the home of Texas A&M, there has been a 55 percent increase in the minority population and a 5 percent increase in Democratic votes.[28] Bell County, which includes the diverse population from the huge U.S. Army installation at Fort Hood, has seen an 8 percent increase in Democratic votes in the same period. These trends are seen in one of the most conservative counties in the state—Collin County outside Dallas—where the Democratic base vote in presidential election years is getting close to 40 percent. These areas, previously ignored by recent statewide Democratic candidates, provide fertile ground for a serious, well-targeted, smart messaging campaign in off years. If the "presidential" Democrats and new minority residents could be persuaded to vote in off-year state and local elections, Democrats would significantly improve their chances of winning statewide.

With the Republican suburban base vote diminishing, the "Texas Way" could one day take on a new meaning. It has already happened in what was once the most reactionary Republican city in Texas.

How Dallas Became a Democratic Stronghold

Democratic activist Lisa Turner remembers being shocked and surprised when she noticed something fundamentally different about Dallas County voting patterns in the 2004 general election. Voters, generally considered conservative and socked away in the Republican column for years, elected a Democrat for county sheriff. What's more, new sheriff Lupe Valdez was female, Hispanic, and a lesbian. What was going on? How did Lupe Valdez win?

Turner got her start in politics running a volunteer phone bank for Ann Richards in Denton County in 1990, and she had been involved in dozens of Democratic campaigns since then. She had just come out of veteran Democratic congressman Martin Frost's losing campaign for reelection. Tom DeLay's slash-and-burn, kill-off-the-Democrats redistricting scheme had taken special aim at Frost, who had been head of the Democratic Congressional Campaign Committee (DCCC) and was widely considered a master tactician in the U.S. House. Frost ended up in a conservative congressional district held by Republican incumbent Pete Sessions. Although an underdog from the beginning, Frost spent more than $3 million and waged an intensive campaign among Anglo voters in North Dallas. His efforts managed to produce a significant number of crossover Republican votes, but he was unable to pull off a win.

Dallas County had been such safe territory for Republicans since the 1970s that Democrats didn't even field a complete slate of candidates in 2004 to challenge their dominance. The local Democratic Party was in disarray, broke, and riddled with rivalries and dissention. No one, including Lisa Turner, gave any Democratic candidate, much less Lupe Valdez, a chance to win. Texas county sheriffs were usually composed of the macho, beer-bellied, tough-talking, cowboy-hat crowd, and since the 1990s few of them had been Democrats. Valdez was obviously different—the youngest of seven children of migrant farm laborers, a former captain in the U.S. Army, and after 9/11 a special investigative agent with the new Department of Homeland Security. Valdez's win was so unique that it made national headlines because Texas had somehow elected the first openly lesbian Hispanic sheriff in the country.

To understand how it happened, Turner and Matt Angle, who had been Martin Frost's chief of staff and at one time staff director for the DCCC, pored over the countywide election results.

White Republicans were continuing their trek to the suburbs, and the void was being filled by African Americans and Hispanics. Although Turner and others knew that demographic shifts would ultimately favor Democrats, they didn't expect it to show up so soon. But there were other changes as well.

As early as 1993 Dallas had openly gay members on its city council. By 1995, the city had stopped its discriminatory hiring practices against members of the LGBT community. Several Dallas neighborhoods, like the bustling Oak Lawn area, had large gay enclaves, and by 2004 same-sex couples were buying homes all over Dallas. Some of the shifting residential patterns within the LGBT communities could possibly account for the fact that sheriff-elect Valdez had drawn support throughout the city.

Looking deeper into the 2004 results, it was clear that the primary reason that Lupe Valdez won was that there had been a 10,000-vote drop-off among Republicans from candidates at the top of the ballot to those at the bottom—and the sheriff's race was near the bottom of the ballot. In Texas during general elections, voters can punch one button or pull one lever and vote a straight ticket for the entire Republican or Democratic Party slate. Alternatively, voters may go through the entire ballot to cast individual votes for a Republican here or a Democrat there, or for a rare independent candidate who might show up on the ballot. In 2004, for the first time in years, the Democratic straight-ticket voters outnumbered Republicans 51 to 48 percent, a margin of 3 percent. Many of those Republicans who had crossed over to vote for Martin Frost simply did not finish their ballots or even vote in the sheriff's race. The Republican vote drop-off was also the reason that Democrats picked up three judgeships in the over-whelmingly GOP judiciary. When this information was com-bined with the fact that in his own hometown President George W. Bush pulled barely 50 percent in his reelection campaign against John Kerry's 49 percent, it was clear that Dallas County was ready for change.

Turner and Angle figured out that if they could pull together the resources to actually recruit candidates to compete for all of-fices, and bring a significant number of 2004 voters back to the polls in the 2006 off-year elections, they might have a chance to revive the moribund Democratic Party. Fortunately, they had a rich angel who was willing to bankroll the effort.

Money–It's Always the Money!

Matt Angle and Lisa Turner were not the only Democratic activ-ists who viewed the 2004 election results with fresh eyes. Marc Stanley, a successful Dallas lawyer who had been a key supporter of Ann Richards, a major fund-raiser for national Democrats, and later would head the National Jewish Democratic Council, had taken his own look at the numbers. In conversations with Angle, who was trying to figure out a game plan for 2006, Stan-ley suggested that Angle go see trial lawyer Fred Baron, whose interest was also piqued by the surprising 2004 results. Baron and his lawyer wife, Lisa Blue, had also been major donors to Ann Richards and had a long history of significant financial support for Democrats all over the country. Baron had won billions of dollars for clients in asbestos cases and became enormously successful representing victims of toxic and chemical exposure. After he sold his interest in his law firm in 2002, Baron spent most of his time raising money for Democrats across the nation. He served as finance chair for his longtime friend John Edwards's campaign before co-chairing the Kerry Victory '04 Committee, a joint effort of the Democratic National Committee and Kerry's presidential campaign.

Matt Angle recalls that when he presented a plan to Baron for a local effort in 2006, he asked three basic questions: What will you do? Why will you do it? And why do you think it will work? When Angle successfully answered the questions, Baron put up the first $1 million to set up the Texas Democratic Trust. This new entity would focus on building a viable political structure in Dallas as well concentrate on winning some key races to close the gap between Republicans and Democrats in the state house.[29]

Earlier in 2004 attorney Russell Langley had created another Democratic political action committee, called the Texas Values in Action Coalition (TexVAC). Langley had once organized a group called Aggies for Ann when he was an undergraduate at Texas A&M University; he had also served a stint as executive director of the Dallas County Democratic Party.[30]

It bothered Langley to see more than $7 million from Dallas donors go to national Democratic candidates in 2000 and 2002. It didn't surprise him, however, because he had learned from his own experience that big donors preferred to send their dollars to Democrats who might win elections nationally, rather than to the dysfunctional local party. He hoped that a separate organization to help Democrats might keep some of that money in Dallas. Langley had also watched the changing demographics and noticed that as early as 2002, a single Democratic candidate for a district judgeship had broken through the all-Republican judiciary to win. Believing that there might be new opportunities ahead, he was able to raise a small amount of money to support several Democratic candidates in 2004. He got his first check for $1,000 from prominent donor Cecilia Boone, who, along with her husband, Garrett, had co-founded the Container Store. By 2005, TexVAC was raising a respectable amount of money, and Langley's venture became an integral part of the Texas Democratic Trust's core group of like-minded organizations.

One of the first actions of the new groups in early 2005 was to hire a big advertising firm to figure out what was going on with self-identified Democratic voters as well as Republicans and independents. The surprising finding was how isolated white Democrats felt in Republican Dallas. They knew so few other Democrats that they were often embarrassed to tell friends and neighbors that they voted Democratic. Many of them felt so hopeless about Democratic prospects in Dallas that they rarely voted except in presidential elections. TexVAC then organized a small public-relations effort to instill a bit of pride and hope among white Democratic voters. Working with the Democratic Trust and another group founded by Matt Angle, the Lone Star Project, the joint effort began to identify these fall-off voters for a major targeting effort in 2006.[31]

Armed with a plan and significant funding, Angle and Turner recruited Jane Hamilton to run a newly constituted Dallas GOTV program. Hamilton was a dynamic African American activist who had once worked in Austin for Dallas state representative Helen Giddings. Hamilton had recently gone to Washington to work for Public Strategies, the firm founded by Ann Richards's old friend and confidant Jack Martin.

"Jane was the perfect person to run the program," says Russell Langley. "She was smart, disciplined, and had the courage to tell people 'no' if they wanted to spend money or move into areas not essential to winning specific targeted voters."

The aim was to pump up African American turnout to at least 21 percent of the total vote and to increase Latino turnout to about 7 percent of the total. Even with these numbers, Democrats would still need to get 34 percent of Anglo voters to win, instead of the usual 30 percent they had been getting in recent elections.

To meet these goals, Hamilton and Turner developed a microtargeting program to focus on individual voters wherever they might live, instead of relying only on the kinds of blanket GOTV efforts in minority neighborhoods that Democrats always conducted. "It was a very simplified version of what constitutes most microtargeting today," Angle remembers. "But it worked."

Even as early as 2004, African American voters were no longer bunched up in traditionally black South Dallas neighborhoods. They had begun to move into Republican-leaning North Dallas, and they had also spread into western parts of the county between Dallas and Fort Worth. Hamilton organized paid canvassers and phone banks to go after those voters. With sufficient funds provided by the Trust, TexVAC, and local candidates who pitched in for a coordinated campaign, the groups were able to run a multilayered targeting effort, using mail, door-to-door canvassing, and phone banks, plus a limited amount of cable television time. State senator Royce West, who represented a good chunk of black precincts in South Dallas, cut a cable TV spot aimed at African American viewers and raised funds to air it.

In one of the final meetings with Fred Baron a week before the November 2006 election, Angle said Baron asked him and Hamilton what they thought would happen. "I was hesitant to guess, but I told Fred that we might win half of our races. But Jane said, 'No, we are going to win all of them.'" Hamilton was the central figure in the Dallas campaign, and she knew on a daily basis exactly what was happening among her targeted voters. As a result, her Election Day prediction was right on the money.

"We had seen some evidence of trends earlier, and we thought we would have a shot here and there—maybe win about half of our races," Lisa Turner said. "What we didn't know at the time was that the key to winning half was the same key to winning all."[32]

Democrats won 42 offices—every contested race they took on. They elected an African American district attorney, a liberal county treasurer, and decimated the Republican judiciary—winning every judicial race in which they had a candidate. The Dallas County courthouse was filled with Democratic elected officials for the first time since the mid-1980s, and most of them were liberals—not like the old-style conservative Democrats who fled to the Republican Party when it looked like that was the only game in town.

The Democratic Trust, TexVAC, and a greatly revived local Democratic Party, plus re-energized labor union activists, reached their goals. It was the first well-coordinated GOTV effort since the Ann Richards victory 16 years earlier. The campaign met its Hispanic turnout goals; exceeded the African American turnout projections, and came up with 33 percent of white voters, when they had hoped for 34 percent. Increased Democratic straight-ticket voting more than made up for the 1 percent shortfall in the Anglo vote. Democrats now had a 15,000-vote advantage over straight-ticket Republican voters.

While Hamilton and Turner were focused on Dallas races, Angle and other staff of the Texas Democratic Trust concentrated on finding marginal Republican legislative seats that they might pick off with the right Democratic candidate. "We had to target those districts using our heads, not our hearts," Angle remembers. As a result of this disciplined approach, Angle and the trust drew a lot of heat and resentment from some Democrats and consul-tants who wanted to tap into the trust's funds for their favorite candidates. That did not happen. Instead, the trust put money into the state Democratic Party and the Texas House Democratic Campaign Committee for specific projects in races that were winnable. Again the results were positive. Democrats picked up five legislative seats and narrowed the gap between Republicans and Democrats in the state house of representatives. There were only six more Republicans than Democrats in the house for the 2007 legislative session, and there was new hope that Democrats could take back the legislature in 2008. But, of course, 2008 was a presidential election year, and thanks to the intense Republican aversion to Barack Obama and the help of yet another redistricting triumph, the GOP erased the Democrats' 2006 legislative gains. The miracle was that Democrats in Dallas County held on. The new structure remained intact.

Those strategies, tactics, and organizational efforts have held up well over the years. Dallas County has gone Democratic in every election since 2006. African American turnout has never been below 24 percent of the total vote, and it bumped up to 27 percent for Obama in 2012.

Over the course of the five-year existence of the Texas Democratic Trust, Baron and a small number of other donors put about $12 million into carefully targeted campaigns. The money never went directly to candidates, but to other Democratic organizations engaged in specific strategic research and GOTV projects. The process ensured that trust-funded projects started with a sound strategy, clear goals, and specific proven tactics to meet those goals. It was strategy first, based on real numbers, then tactics—not the other way around.

The Democratic Trust ceased to exist in 2008 after Baron died of a rare blood cancer at the age of 61. His widow, Lisa Blue, continued to put more than $1 million into similar efforts to help individual Democratic candidates. But until the 2014 election cycle, when Steve and Amber Mostyn emerged as Wendy Davis's megadonors and became the primary source of funds for the ill-fated Battleground Texas operation, no other individual Democratic donor has emerged to do what Fred Baron did. Now the money comes in smaller chunks, but the mechanism that produces results in Dallas is still in place.

The Dallas turnaround was the result of critical thinking based on solid analysis to provide evidence that change was possible. It came about because leaders were able to look at old problems in new ways. They had sufficient funds to hire a disciplined manager who knew what to do and how to keep close tabs on every activity and every dollar. Dallas Democrats were so hungry for a victory that they were able to put aside old turf wars and ancient grievances. Yes, they had the benefit of demographic change, but they figured out how to make it work for them—sooner, rather than later.

Too good to be true? Not at all. And it might give Democrats a model for future elections.

TEN

Memo to the Future

IF I WERE STILL A TEXAS POLITICAL OPERA-
tive—a player in the game with sophisticated analytics, boundless
energy, unlimited resources and a Democratic candidate for governor savvy enough to understand we needed a new game plan—I'd
write one of those long memos that I used to prepare for Ann
Richards.

I'm not that kind of player anymore, couldn't be even if I
wanted to. I was never much of a tactician, anyway, only a writer
who synthesized the facts and ideas floating around and put them
into some sort of organized plan for action. In a weird sort of way, I
also actually enjoyed managing people and carrying out a plan that
could bring order from chaos. That was "my thing."

The focus of the memo I want to write is the race for governor.
That is where the process of turning Texas blue has to begin, at
the top. Of course, the U.S. Senate is always a possibility for the
right Democrat at the right time, particularly if Senator Ted Cruz
self-destructs between now and 2018. Democrats also need to peel

away the Republican layers of control over the legislature, an important facet of turning Texas blue. But the governor's office is the big prize. It is the key to returning Texas to political sanity.

I don't have the candidate now or the resources to jump-start a campaign this year or next, but I'm going to write that memo anyway. Presumptuous? Yes. Opinionated? You bet! Out on a shaky limb? Obviously. Most of us who love politics always throw ourselves into shaky ventures. That's what makes it exciting. An intense political campaign can narrow our focus and shut out normal life. It can be an addictive experience: a rush so thrilling when we win, but so deadly exhausting when we lose.

Many years ago, I decided to remove the political blinders that blocked out the rest of the world. I wanted a clearer, less biased view of life. It is not that I didn't care about what happened to the causes that had engaged me for so many years. I just wanted a different way to approach them. I'm hoping that years of experience outside of the political arena in my more normal world of family and work will provide a new perspective to promote the causes I still care about.

I do admit to a kind of crazy hope. I just hope that I'm a little more wily now, with a tendency to be more realistic than before. So here are a few ideas about how to loosen the GOP's grip on America's reddest state.

Dear Texas Democrats . . .

First, let's get the numbers out of the way. Let's use the analytics as a backdrop for all that we do, but not as the only factor to consider.

If we don't get the numbers right, we don't have a chance to win on any other front.

This is what we know:

We have to begin winning at least 35 percent of the white vote statewide to be competitive. That's a big jump from the 25 percent that Wendy Davis got in 2014. I believe it is doable. If we are lucky—and luck will obviously play a part in all that we do—the 2016 presidential election might help us along. If we presume that Hillary Clinton, or some other relatively appealing Democratic presidential nominee, campaigns on issues that matter to centrist voters, it might be possible to draw up to 30 percent of the white vote in Texas. If that were to happen, then the margin for Republicans over Democrats could dip into the single digits, say, a seven- or eight-point advantage. These numbers would not be impossible to overcome in future elections.

Although Barack Obama lost Texas in 2008 and 2012, he carried the African American vote by 98 percent. He got a paltry 26 percent of the white vote. If he had managed to win more than 30 percent of the white vote, as he did in Virginia, Florida, and North Carolina, and if he had invested heavily in a GOTV effort as he did in those states, he might have won Texas too. Hard to believe, isn't it? If the 2016 Democratic presidential candidate attracts more white Texas voters than Obama did, Democrats would have a larger pool to begin wooing for the 2018 statewide campaigns. There are a lot of "ifs" here, I admit. We just have to keep reminding ourselves that white voters make up about two-thirds of the total electorate in off-year elections, and no Democrat since Ann Richards in the 1990s has succeeded in reaching them.

We Democrats still have to increase our vote totals among our base. That means reaching the 65 percent threshold with Hispanic voters, keeping 95 percent of African American voters, and winning Asian, millennial, and new urban voters who are more in tune with the values and issues of the Democratic Party than with the crazy extremists who hold power in Texas today. So if we can pump up the raw numbers among our solid base of Democratic voters (who can be easily identified after the 2016 presidential election), these are the percentages we need to reach in 2018:

Hispanics—65 percent
African Americans—95 percent
Anglos—35 percent

This is not big news to anyone who studies Texas politics. The larger issue is *how* to do it. That's always the rub—not what, but how. Here are ten ways to begin.

1. Find the Right Leader

We've come a long distance from the old Texas Way, but Texans still gravitate to leaders with big personalities who have a strong sense of self that is reflected in their pride, independence, and directness. It probably helps to have a little swagger too.

Don't take this the wrong way. I'm an old-style feminist who believes that swagger is not gender-specific, but simply reflects self-confidence and willingness to take big risks. What we need is a man or woman who has enough self-awareness to understand what is involved in real leadership—building relationships with followers based on trust, vision, honesty, and competence. It has to be natural.

Remember the brashness of old Bill Clements and the Texas twang of truth-telling Ann Richards? Both had swagger. Both had big personalities. Both could inspire followers to move along with them, and neither was too concerned with the political correctness of their day. You knew they were willing to get in your face if they thought you were wrong about policy or politics. Each in very different ways was able to move outside of their party constituencies to create diverse coalitions of voters. Richards courted Republican women. Clements went after Reagan Democrats. They couldn't be boxed into traditional party expectations, and because they were big personalities, they had magnetic qualities that attracted outsiders.

Part of Rick Perry's dominance in Texas after 2004 was the fact that he, too, was a big personality—he had swagger and blunt talk, as well as a willingness to use power to face down political enemies. Texas voters, whatever their circumstance, seem to like that kind of rawness in their politicians. It gives them confidence in their own future. We Democrats didn't like Perry's raw appeal, but Texas voters sure did. Sad to say for Democrats, for all of her intelligence and grasp of key Texas policy issues, Wendy Davis is not a big personality. Of course, neither is Greg Abbott, who defeated her so soundly. When everything seems equally dull, you have a notoriously low-turnout election, as we did in 2014. That is when a well-run, adequately funded campaign matters most.

I'm obviously looking for a Super Democrat. And my Super Democrat will have to rise above the damaged brand of our party, which has been fundamentally discredited after 25 years of harsh, largely unanswered attacks. The brand is sour. It has to be sweetened, and that may require our candidate to have one of those pivotal "Sister Souljah moments" to face down some absurdity within the Democratic Party that would drive away swing voters.[1] When Bill Clinton denounced the black racism that ran through the lyrics of a rap singer named Sister Souljah, he proved to centrist voters that he was not a captive of the political correctness of an increasingly sensitive Democratic Party. He was independent. Texas's Super Democrat has to have the same kind of independence to rise above party labels.

Our ideal leader will not be—cannot be—a new incarnation of Ann Richards, who was a product of her time and set of unique circumstances. The Super Democrat will have to create his or her own set of unique circumstances and make them relevant to a broad swath of Texas's diverse population.

Party leaders are going to have to do a lot of soul searching to settle on a Super Democrat, and that involves asking some decidedly uncomfortable—and politically incorrect—questions. Is state representative Richard Raymond correct when he worries that it might be in the 2020s before his party can be viable enough to elect a Hispanic governor? Do Democrats need an Anglo bridge candidate in the 2018 off-year election who can appeal to enough white voters to break their knee-jerk Republican voting patterns? And if so, who is on the scene that might fill that role? At the same time, Democratic leaders should be recruiting and funding strong Hispanic candidates for key statewide offices that could give promising men and women opportunities for leadership now and in the future. Democrats have to wrestle with these issues in an honest, straightforward discussion. That's the only way for the best answer and the right leaders to emerge.

2. Find the Path to Reach White Voters

In 2014, Texas Democrats were able to pull only 25 percent of the white vote. But this was not only a Texas problem. In almost every contested election across the country in which a Democratic candidate for governor or U.S. senator lost, white voters were missing.

Former governor of Tennessee Phil Bredesen hit the nail on the head when he told party leaders, "If you have a product that's not working, you don't say, 'our customers are lazy' or 'our customers don't know what's best for them.'"[2] But that's what Democrats have been saying in Texas for years . . . we'd win if only *our* voters would just vote! Enough of that. If we were in the business world and had been losing market share because of ineffective advertising for the same old unpopular product, we'd be saying that we need a better product and a different communications strategy. A better "product" for Texas would be a stronger candidate, an all-encompassing strategy, a more relevant message, and a more effective structure to reach white voters.

Václav Havel, the renowned writer and Czech dissident who became president of the new Czech Republic after the fall of the Soviet Union, used to talk about a "rule of everydayness."[3] The old Soviet system had little understanding or concern about how ordinary people lived each day, and it was one of the failures of a system that was more concerned with ideology—in a way, a more authoritarian form of political correctness—than with how people actually lived.

We need to start asking ourselves: What is the rule of every-dayness for white Texans who are not in the top 10 percent of the wealthiest people in our state? What are the concerns about their families or their homes or their safety? What kinds of bills pile up every month? How are they going to manage the cost of higher education for their children? While Democrats, to their credit, have made an effort to understand the rule of everydayness for those left out of life's bounties, they often write off the concerns of those who don't necessarily live on the edges of life, but are stuck somewhere in the muddled middle, where problems still exist and struggles still matter.

Middle-class suburban moms worry about their teenagers experimenting with drugs as much as moms in poor inner-city neighborhoods do.

Middle-class families worry about putting their aged and infirm parents into inferior nursing homes as much as poor families do.

Single moms in suburban neighborhoods worry about child care, wage stagnation, and escalating rents, as do single moms everywhere.

Middle-class suburban families fret about traffic congestion, poor air quality, boarded-up shopping centers, and a whole lot of other issues that could be addressed by state officials—if they weren't so busy trying to please Tea Party fanatics rather than or-dinary folks, even those who live in suburbs.

When I look at the structure of the Democratic Party in Texas today, with all of its committees and special-interest caucuses, I see a big, fat void. We've got a dozen different caucuses for every imaginable group: several for women as well as for African Ameri-cans and Hispanics. Others are for Asians, environmentalists,

LGBTQ activists, those with disabilities, organized labor, teachers, and more. But there is not a single caucus or interest group that focuses on the concerns or needs of suburban Texas communities, where millions of white voters live. It is as if they don't exist, or that people who live there don't worry about schools, jobs, property taxes, transportation, adequate water supplies, escalating insurance premiums, soaring electric power rates, or anything else that might constitute their "rule of everydayness."

Suburban white voters are not on the radar of the Democratic Party of Texas. The message comes across loud and clear at election time.

"It passes my understanding how, particularly in the past few years, we've ignored the economic pain that's been created in this country," said Bredesen when he admonished Democrats to focus on economic issues that constrain middle-income suburbanites, as well as the working poor.[4]

Democratic candidates from top to bottom could be shouting out issues that matter to white voters, using mail, social media, canvassing, and community meetings to reach new voters. They could bring up key questions that suburban voters want answered, such as:

Who is responsible when Texas law allows insurance companies to deny your claims for roof damage after one of our violent spring storms?

Who is responsible when our state allows a driller to put a rig for hydraulic fracking a hundred yards from your front door?

Who is responsible when the local nursing home closes in your small town because the legislature cut support for state medical facilities, and you have to move your 90-year-old mother to a facility 50 miles away?

We know that Republicans in the Texas legislature and the governor's office are responsible for these and other issues that concern many Anglo voters. But do the voters know? Little insurrections bubble up all the time in the suburbs, and many could be used to woo white voters.

To reach the 35 percent threshold of white voters, Democrats can no longer ignore the issues that matter to them.

3. Distinguish Between Vision and Message

The great dancer and choreographer Twyla Tharp always creates a central theme, a big idea that is the organizing principle for her works. She has called the idea her "spine." Everything in the dance flows from the spine, the structure that holds it all together. It is revealed subtly in the lighting, the music, the visual backdrop, the rhythm and timing of movement and interplay of the dancers.[5] I think Democrats would benefit from considering how we choreograph a campaign that flows from its spine, its big idea, and its vision.

What is our big idea? Why do we want to turn Texas blue in the first place? Is it so that our Democratic friends can hold elective offices and help with our pet projects? Do we simply want to avoid the embarrassment of loose cannons like Louie Gohmert or the absurdity of a small-minded governor who orders law enforcement to monitor federal military training exercises so that American soldiers don't take over our homes or schools? Of course, there is nothing wrong with being against stupidity. That's not a bad motivation, but it is not enough to change Texas.

We need to go a bit deeper as a party and as individuals who want to lead it. We have to distinguish between the game of winning and the substance of vision and policy. What do we want Texas to be like by 2025? How can we fund public schools at a level to keep classes small enough for kids to learn and teachers to teach? How do we intend keep the Texas economy strong and have good-paying jobs available to allow people to move into the middle class? What kinds of technological innovations would make our roads safer and our air cleaner? How could we really begin to create an "infrastructure of opportunity," instead of just talking about it? We don't need any more planks in a Democratic Party platform that satisfies all of our constituent groups. We just need some serious thinking about the future of Texas and its people.

More than 40 years ago, Royal Dutch Shell started a strategic vision development initiative led in later years by Texan Joe Jaworski, son of famed Watergate prosecutor Leon Jaworski. The process involved the amalgamation of facts and credible data projections about economic, political, environmental, social, and cultural changes that were already under way and expected to continue. Then Shell developed several scenarios projecting best- and worst-case events, written in a narrative, almost storylike form, that clearly laid out for non-experts what the future might hold if they took various kinds of actions or simply did nothing at all. From these scenarios, Shell officials gleaned enough information to come up with their big idea and choose the best path to achieve their goals. Variations on Shell's scenario process have since been used by numerous international organizations, the U.S. military, and major businesses throughout the world. Maybe Texas Democrats would benefit from such a process.

As far back as 2002, former Texas state demographer Steve Murdock, whom George W. Bush later named as head of the U.S. Census Bureau, compiled an analysis of population projections through 2040 to indicate what might happen in Texas if the state did not start paying attention to its schools, its infrastructure, its in-migration patterns, and the downward trending economic indicators for its growing minority populations. Based on trends in the early 2000s, he noted that if serious changes were not under way by 2020, Texas could face a bleak future by 2040. Texas would not only be more ethnically diverse than the rest of the nation, it would also be older, poorer, less educated, and less healthy. But without a significant investment in people and schools, Texans both old and young would need increased public and private assistance, requiring massive expenditures. Murdock suggested that the year 2020 might be the tipping point for Texas: either change direction or face a more dismal future for the majority of its population.[6] Not much has happened since 2002 to alter his projections.

A smart, independent-minded Democratic candidate could use information from this kind of data to create a vision to inspire change.

People have a way of imagining their own lives—how and who they want to be, and what they want for their families and their communities. The right candidate who takes on the responsibility to lead must articulate the kind of vision in which people can imagine a brighter future for Texas that is in sync with their own dreams.

Ann Richards and her team had a vision for a New Texas. Sure, it sounded corny at times, and its implementation was full of flaws. But it conveyed a set of values and an imaginative vision of the future where the doors of opportunity would be open to all Texans. This vision was specific enough in a hard-fought campaign to allow people to see how it could happen. It fit the times, the circumstances, and the aspirations of millions of Texans, and its simple two-word phrase revealed Richards's beliefs and intentions for change. The right Texas leader will bring forward a vision that is authentic for the Texas of today.

4. Develop a Strategy to Win

Think strategy, not tactics. This is my mantra. We cannot mistake tactical calculations for strategic thinking, as we have tended to do since Ann Richards lost in 1994. Yes, we will establish key goals—the percentage of white votes we need to win, the number of Hispanic votes we must hold, the desire to maintain African American loyalty, the development of the youth vote, the incorporation of gay, lesbian, and transgendered Texans into our cause. None of that is new to our Democratic friends.

What we have to do differently is figure out *how* to reach those goals in very specific ways. That's where strategy begins. It is a whole system approach based on accurate analytics that determine specific tactics that go into a plan, a budget, and a timetable based on facts, not hopes. Properly understood, a campaign budget should be a strategic document that funds priorities, measures results, and ensures that adequate funds are available when needed. Sounds easy. Simple common sense, no doubt.

Yet why did the Wendy Davis campaign run out of money two months before Election Day? While the campaign had goals, it did not have a strategy that meshed with a comprehensive budget that could ration scarce resources within a timetable to carry out a plan. No money for broadcast or cable media in the final week? No money for direct mail or canvassing of swing voters? No money for paid canvassers to supplement volunteers? Pity! The campaign did have a set of get-out-the-vote tactics, but they were based on erroneous assumptions, flawed data, and unrealistic expectations. A bold tactical effort can never rescue an inadequate plan. Didn't work then, won't work now.

The most important time in a political campaign can be before it ever begins. That is when the candidate and consultants can be most creative, most logical, and most data-driven to organize a winning effort. That is when ideas are tested, when resources are identified, and timetables can be organized. That is when all of the aspects of the campaign can be shaped into a coherent whole that can serve as the road map when the action becomes fast and furious. Any campaign that shaves time at the outset will be in serious trouble at the end.

5. Assume the Role of a Republican Strategist

So we have a great candidate, a clear vision, a realistic strategy, and a detailed plan using current data and good analytics. What could possibly go wrong? Think like a Republican and you will see. Why not assume the role of a Republican strategist and plan the kind of campaign Republicans would use to defeat us?

Nothing will be more likely to save Democrats from the kinds of erroneous assumptions that sunk Wendy Davis than to figure out what the Republicans might do to win their own campaign.

Two of the most recent Democratic campaigns for governor—Bill White in 2010 and Wendy Davis in 2014—saw an unexpected barrage of attack ads and mailings in the last three weeks of the campaign. White, even with the odds against him, didn't really lose the race until Rick Perry outspent him three to one in his home base of Houston and ran brutal attack ads, destroying his credibility with longtime Anglo supporters and suppressing the heavy African American turnout he had counted on. Perry hit White on illegal immigration, his ties to the Obama administration, and his financial dealings before becoming mayor—he simply took the shine off White's remarkable record. "White had to do well in Houston and Perry just destroyed him there. It was a block-and-tackle campaign, surgical and well-organized," one consultant remembered. Because the attacks came so late—and there were so many of them on different hot-button issues—they were hard to refute with the limited funds available.

In the last month of the race, after some of her campaign operatives bragged to the media and donors that Davis was surging in internal polls, the Republican TV onslaught against her began in earnest. While Abbott's campaign probably didn't need to hit so hard because their own polling showed Davis already running double digits behind, the scathing attack ads ran everywhere. They charged Davis with unproven conflicts of interests resulting from what they claimed were secretive business dealings and legislative favors for clients in her law practice. Probably the most damaging charge against her, however, was that she was an Obama pawn who was going to take her marching orders from Washington.

That should have been no surprise! Even as far back as George W. Bush's win against Ann Richards in 1994, the Republicans stoked fear in the final weeks of the campaign among rural and small-town residents all over East Texas. The counties along the Louisiana border had traditionally been a stable base of Democratic voters and had gone for Richards in 1990. But the Bush operatives were all over East Texas, and anti-gay rhetoric picked up steam in the final month of the campaign. Republican state senator Bill Ratliff from Tyler, who was an honorary chair of the Bush campaign, told news reporters that he was against Richards's appointment of "avowed homosexual activists . . . to positions of leadership," providing attack fodder to anti-gay preachers throughout the area.[7]

I remember getting a call during the campaign's final week from a friend in Lufkin telling me about inflammatory spots on Christian talk radio ranting about the godless homosexuals in the governor's office. Flyers were also showing up on car windows of Sunday churchgoers claiming that Ann was going to confiscate their guns. It all seemed so ludicrous, I couldn't imagine that anyone would believe the lies. Yet when those flyers, mailings, and radio spots saturated the area, Democratic votes just evaporated.

I'm embarrassed to admit that I was surprised. Why didn't we expect such an attack? We simply never made a shrewd assessment of what an intense Republican effort among small-town and rural voters in East Texas might unleash at a point in the campaign when there was too little time to mount an effective counterattack.

Any serious Democrat who emerges to challenge Republicans for high office in 2018 can expect the same or worse. The best way to prepare for such attacks is to ensure that someone who thinks like a Republican vets the candidate. What will a Republican see that a Democrat might not? How might something a Democrat might be proud of be turned around and used as an attack? What is the most devastating information that could emerge near the end of the campaign? How and when might it be defused? Only someone with a Republican mind-set will know.

One reason George W. Bush waged such effective campaigns for president in 2000 and 2004 was that two former Democrats were part of his inner circle—Matthew Dowd and Mark McKinnon. Although Karl Rove got the credit, they, not Rove, drove the campaign strategy and message. Dowd understood the numbers and the Electoral College strategy it would take to win, as Rove did not, and McKinnon understood that a centrist message was the way to win votes from Middle Americans. They thought like Democrats, knew how to appeal to swing voters, and provided an enormous advantage by holding the line against some of the right-wingers who surrounded Bush. Let's find our version of Dowd and McKinnon. We may need them.

6. Drop the Hype

This suggestion is short and sweet, and maybe a bit sour as well. Do not raise initial expectations to extraordinary heights. Do not hype the internal workings of your campaign wizardry. In 2014, the intensity of the backlash against Battleground Texas might not have been so brutal had expectations not been so high. Jeremy Bird and his staff came into Texas with a stack of press releases about how they were going to transform Texas in the next two election cycles. If there had been a strong Davis campaign manager at the time with a clear line of authority, that kind of talk could have been quashed immediately. Don't broadcast internal polling numbers. Don't brag about what you're going to do. Just do it.

7. Run a Whole-State Campaign

Texas has 254 counties. In recent elections Democrats have focused on only six big ones, plus the Rio Grande Valley. There are at least 50 additional counties in Texas that have blocs of minority voters, as well as white voters who might be lured back to voting Democratic. So go where no Democrat has gone since Ann Richards ran for governor. Go everywhere!

Republican Bill Clements ran a 254-county campaign and ventured into strange new territory for a Republican. George W. Bush left safe Republican areas to make a major push deep into East Texas, which had been Democratic territory in 1990.

Democrats have not ventured into new areas in almost 20 years. It will be difficult to shake the conventional wisdom in our party that all we have to do is to work harder to get out the base vote in the big cities and the Valley. But Democrats have the potential to expand their base vote in at least 29 mid-size cities throughout Texas, as well as to pick up disaffected moderate Republicans in key suburbs.

Dr. James Henson, who runs the Texas Politics Project at the University of Texas at Austin and conducts regular polls for the online *Texas Tribune*, estimates that 20 to 30 percent of Texas's moderate Republicans might be open to voting for the right Democrat under the right conditions in the right kind of election.[8] They just have to be identified and bombarded with relevant issues and effective tactics. To do so on a whole-state level will take resources: money and people. It will also take a candidate who can lead the party—against years of resistance—and understand that this is the first step toward rebuilding the Democratic Party as a viable institution in Texas.

8. Connect the Dots Between Policies and Politics

In 2014, Denton, just north of Dallas, became the first city in Texas to ban the practice of fracking within its city limits. Fracking, or hydraulic fracturing, is the process of injecting water, sand, and chemicals underground to extract oil and gas from shale formations. Denton, with a population of about 125,000, has been the epicenter of the practice because it sits atop the gas-rich Barnett shale formation that stretches across 24 North Texas counties. Natural gas extracted from shale formations is a cleaner fuel source than coal. But the process of extracting it has, so far, created other problems. In Denton, after major oil companies put their rigs near residential areas and local schools, residents began to complain about poor air and water quality, as well as disruptive noise from drilling, heavy truck traffic in residential neighborhoods, and even an increase in low-magnitude earthquakes.

A local citizens group gathered sufficient signatures to get a proposed ordinance banning fracking within city limits on the November ballot. They won the election by a margin of

59 percent to 41 percent, despite the almost $700,000 that oil companies had spent to defeat it. Yet the day after the election, Texas Railroad Commissioner Christi Craddick, one of the three elected Republicans who run the agency that oversees oil and gas production, announced that the agency would not honor the town's vote to ban fracking, and the practice would continue. Adding insult to injury for Denton residents, the Republican majority in the 2015 legislature passed a law that forced Denton to repeal its anti-fracking ordinance. The new law also prohibited other Texas cities from stopping fracking in their communities. Governor Greg Abbott signed the new law with great fanfare. But here's the disconnect: Denton also voted overwhelmingly for Abbott and the Republican slate of candidates that took away their power to enact certain local ordinances. Wouldn't it be a good idea for a Democratic candidate for governor to go into Denton and blame Greg Abbott and the Republican-controlled legislature for overturning the will of the voters on an issue that really mattered to them?

Credible Democratic candidates—local and statewide—can use issues like this to drive a wedge between local voters and their Republican representatives. It is one way to use voter microtargeting to begin shaving Republican vote totals in their base counties.

There are other issues—even local disasters—that result from lax regulatory policies or failure to respond to desperate community needs. In 2013 a fertilizer plant, where tons of ammonium nitrate were stored, exploded in the small community of West, just north of Waco. The blast from the explosion and resulting fire killed 15 people, injured 160 more, and damaged or destroyed 150 buildings, including the town's middle school, a nursing home, and a 50-unit apartment complex. First-responder volunteer firefighters were among those killed because they entered the burning building without knowing that it contained volatile materials. Incredibly, the fertilizer company had never informed the local fire marshal about the explosive materials, and members of the community had no idea that the plant could be dangerous. Abbott, who was attorney general at the time, refused to order similar facilities to publicly disclose the explosive materials on their sites. Enterprising Texas news reporters dug up the facts anyway.

There are 92 of these fertilizer facilities all across the state, and many are located near homes and schools. Yet two years after the disaster, Texas had made no changes in law, policies, or regulatory measures to protect residents from similar explosions. During a recent inspection by the state fire marshal, only one-fifth of those plants had a sprinkler system to put out a small fire that could cause a major explosion. Fifty-two facilities had no means of fire protection except handheld fire extinguishers, and 22 had no fire protection features at all. Who is responsible?

A savvy candidate in a whole-state campaign could build a compelling case among rural and suburban voters that any Republican who allowed these life-threatening situations to continue should to be thrown out of office. Yes, it will take research, resources, and relevant messages from candidates willing to take this kind of plunge into local issues, but it can be done.

Someone once asked Texas music icon Willie Nelson how he had been able to write so many different kinds of songs. He said that there were millions of melodies floating through the air. You just had to pull them out.

There are a lot of big stories that matter to people floating through the air in Texas. Democrats just have to pull them out and start using them to win voters they have long ignored.

9. Spread the Word About Republican Extremism

Since the mid-1980s in Texas, Republicans have waged war on the Democratic Party brand, and they've done a heck of a job. Of course, they've had national help in doing so. Democrats have been so demonized for so long that in some social circles, it's not quite acceptable to be one. In Texas they've rarely fought back with the ferocity with which they were attacked.

Once, when I made the mistake of going to my high school reunion, one of the "girls" I once knew ran across the room, pointing her finger at me and yelling, "Liberal, liberal, liberal!" That's how it goes sometimes—liberal, labor, lefty, libertine, loose, lax, lazy—the alliterations could go on. We've all heard them, and in the eyes of some Texans they apply to all Democrats (along with dozens of other derogatory phrases). Perhaps the "tax-and-spend" label is hardest to peel away. To many voters in Texas that's all Democrats in Washington ever do: take their money and give it to undeserving bums who turn around and reward Democrats with their votes. To be equated with the national Democratic Party has been the kiss of death for any candidate who had the nerve to run for statewide office. Some consultants and commentators think the brand is so sour that only an independent candidate could begin to take the state away from Republicans. I'm not so sure about that. I think that fighting back is the solution now.

Republican extremism in Texas since 2008 has given Democrats enough ammunition to fight back with gusto and drop the GOP brand into a pot of crazy-hot grease. Isn't it time to call out the crackpots and cranks and make thoughtful Republicans and other normal people feel a little embarrassed to be associated with them? Isn't the best defense a good offense?

It is time to launch a carefully calibrated and well-funded campaign to equate the Republican brand with extremism and reckless behavior that is dangerous to families and communities.

We can't wait to do this until we are in a full-blown election cycle in 2018. I wish we had one of those special-purpose expenditure committees that would pump about $10 million into targeted media efforts that highlight the crazy or corrupt deeds of Texas Republicans. Wait a minute—I just did what Democrats always do: *wish for something to happen!* Let me phrase my sentence a bit differently. Isn't there anyone out there who will put together a group that might take on something like this as a worthy project? Now I'm pleading instead of wishing. But that leads me to my final suggestion.

10. Keep Texas Money in Texas

This is the hard one. While Texas Democrats may never have as much money to spend in campaigns as Texas Republicans, there are still a lot of rich Democrats in this state. They just keep sending their money all over the country to help Democrats in California or Wisconsin or wherever dollars are needed nationally. Even Naomi Aberly, whose notable fund-raising event in 2013 kicked off the money train for Wendy Davis, keeps throwing big soirees for national Democrats to rub shoulders with wealthy Texas liberals, shake their hands, and take their money.

There are as many as 50 wealthy Democrats, probably more, who could write million-dollar checks to help a credible Democrat with a solid strategy run a winning campaign for Texas governor. And there are thousands of Democrats who could—and would—write $100 checks again and again. The Super Democrat who might make a race for governor will have to come up with sufficient seed money to warrant their trust and secure their dollars. More importantly, Democrats who are ready and willing to turn Texas blue have to start *now* to build the financial infrastructure to support—and hasten—the change that can occur.

Well . . . that's it . . . the end of my memo. Now, it's up to you. If you find it useful and are still interested, you could put this summary on your "to-do" list or in your smartphone.

1. Find the right leader.
2. Find the path to reach white voters.
3. Distinguish between vision and message.
4. Develop a winning strategy based on facts.
5. Assume the role of a Republican strategist.
6. Drop the hype.
7. Run a whole-state campaign.
8. Connect the dots between politics and policy.
9. Spread the word about Republican extremism.

10. Keep Texas money in Texas.

This list won't change Texas. That's going to take people with vision, fortitude, and perseverance. Now that I've gotten my two cents in, I'll cheer them on. Texas is ready for them. Texas is ready for change.

Afterword

MY CAMPAIGN EXPERIENCES IN TEXAS ARE now ancient history. To see them in the context of today, it helps to remember the old French proverb: *The more things change, the more they stay the same.* Political campaigns remain pretty much as they've always been—messy, chaotic, and often brutalizing experiences.

In 1990, when I became campaign manager for Ann Richards's first race for governor, an old hand at running campaigns told me, "All you have to do is make decisions." That quickly proved to be an empty promise. It wasn't as if I could loll around reading the news clips and position papers, then show up at a staff meeting to choose from an array of rational options laid out for me by calm, deliberate staffers who had spent their time putting together reasoned proposals for significant action. Many of my days were filled with time-consuming, mind-numbing junk—some of it so stupid that I'm embarrassed to admit how much time I wasted on so many needless distractions.

I took too many calls from a big contributor who hated the finance chairman and wanted to be "in the loop" on key decisions.

I spent too much time trying to smooth the ruffled feathers of a county coordinator who was angry because one of her old enemies got to pick up Ann from the airport and take her to the senior citizens' center. I even had to tell my dad—gently, of course—why we couldn't use the bumper sticker he had designed. I was disturbed by picketers who stood outside my office window holding up signs of aborted fetuses. I worried about the guy going through our garbage bin at night—was he looking for incriminating documents, or merely trying to find leftover food? Then there were the late-night calls from Ann, dragging in from a torturous day on the road and seeking a few words of reassurance before dropping her bones into bed at midnight. Not much time for calm deliberation.

Minor, inconsequential decisions in the overall scheme of things often set off a torrent of complaints—like the agonizing telephone conversations with a few key supporters after I decided to terminate the services of a particularly obnoxious and ineffective fund-raising consultant. I remember a crazy day when I had to placate a state senator who demanded that Ann return to a particular feed store in his district because she had not spent enough time there on an earlier visit. Old friends became media critics who picked apart our carefully crafted television spots. You have to be a slippery, disciplined, and somewhat heartless dictator to win a close, high-stakes campaign. I loved and hated it at the same time.

Today more than ever, campaigns have become the obsession of our "chattering class" of pundits, commentators, consultants, and candidates. But it is boring chatter to most Americans, and they choose not to participate. In 2014, just 36 percent of eligible Americans voted in the off-year elections, the lowest percentage of eligible voters who actually cast a ballot since 1942. In Texas, only about 28 percent of eligible voters came to the polls.[1] Many folks sense the disconnection of incessant campaign chatter from the experience of their day-to-day lives. Why bother to vote? For all of his particular brand of crazy during the Republican primaries for 2016, at least Donald Trump made it interesting.

The challenge for Texas Democrats is to show voters they have a real stake in the outcome. Democrats are right on the issues that really matter to most Texans—health care, income inequality, immigration reform, public-school funding, minimum wage increases, air and water quality, the dangers of our expanding gun culture, and so many others that, if addressed rationally, could improve the lives of ordinary Texans.

America's great orator and public servant Barbara Jordan used to quote Lyndon Johnson when she talked about the role of government. "He saw the enemy, and the enemy was *not* government," she said. "The enemy was ignorance, poverty, disease, ugliness, injustice, and discrimination. He believed that it was the duty of government to defeat the enemy."[2] My fear about Texas's right-wing Republicans is that they are so obsessed with the notion of government-as-enemy that they exhibit a willful indifference to human suffering. Texas Democrats, to their credit, have focused on government as the tool to minimize human suffering. They have just been slow in figuring out how to acquire the political power to do what needs to be done.

For the past few years, politics in Texas has masked the complexities of living in a world already changed dramatically by technology and by extreme disparities among people in both wealth and knowledge. The stresses of these new realities have strained the notion of a common good and a universal set of values necessary to hold together strong communities. In Texas, with the extremists in such firm control, I worry that we have created a class of office-holders who are losing essential, life-affirming human capacities like judgment, common sense, empathy, responsibility, altruism, or even basic honesty. I am concerned that the thoughtlessness that permeates politics today snares even the best and brightest among us. Yet I understand how hard it is, in the heat of battle, to maintain a thoughtful dialogue about what we do and why we do it. When you are in the fight, it is hard to see reality because, as political philosopher Hannah Arendt has written, "Everybody is swept away unthinkingly by what everybody else says and believes in."[3]

When we allow ourselves to stop long enough to question what everybody else is saying and allow common sense to become part of our dialogue, reality hits us in the face. That is when serious thought about the future can begin.

The reality of Texas politics has certainly hit me in the face, as it has thousands of others, both inside and outside of the game. I'm hoping that the blow from the most recent defeats will force us to ask some penetrating questions about everything we try in the future to turn Texas blue. We need to be asking:

What led to this?

What connects this to that?

How do we know what we are told is true . . . or false?

Who prepared the evidence? What is their interest?

What is missing from the analysis? What is another way of looking at this?

Who says what and from what point of view?

Whose problem is it? Will the solution cause more problems? Why would anyone care?

These are the questions I hope Texas Democrats will ask themselves—and any consultant, candidate, donor, or activist who appears on the scene with a magic plan to turn Texas blue.[4]

In preparing for this book, I took note when former U.S. senator Kay Bailey Hutchison told me so emphatically that she did not want to be labeled a "moderate" Republican. She emphasized that she was a true conservative now stranded in the land of right-wing radical ideologues who had captured her party and had mistakenly identified themselves as "conservative." Knowing who you are makes a difference.

All through this book, I have identified myself as an unabashed liberal Democrat in a Texas political world that disdains that label. My bias has always been for the underdog, for those at the bottom of life's heap. I believe in the premise of democracy, that ordinary people have the capacity to think and act responsibly if they are told the truth and not fed a bunch of lies based on fear and manipulation. I believe that government can be an instrument to relieve human misery. I believe that we have responsibilities to each other and to the community we share. I still see politics as the way to put my beliefs into action. And I still think it is important to master the strategies and tactics that allow those with critical habits of thought to win political campaigns in order to shape public policy in a responsive and responsible manner.

The Greek writer Nikos Kazantzakis, best known as the author of *Zorba the Greek,* saw life as a spiral. Within it, powerful forces resisting change always push downward in the swirls of the spiral to prevent hope for the new from rising.[5] In sculpture, we see the expression of this imagery in Michelangelo's *Moses*, whose half-finished form struggles to emerge from the rock. Whether in art, politics, or life, there is always a struggle to bring something new into being. The birth of the new can occur only when upward-moving progressive forces hold the downward reactionary forces in an unsteady, uncomfortable balance on the spiral of life. That's what I want for Texas: balance on the spiral to allow those at the bottom to experience the birth of a new era of hope.

Acknowledgments

WHEN YOU WRITE FROM MEMORY AND EXPE-
rience, there are many people along the way who have shaped your
thinking and shared their wisdom. I could not write a book about
Texas politics without recognizing their influence on my life.

I owe so much to two such individuals, now deceased, who
opened the doors to the world of politics for me. First, my late
husband, John Rogers, taught me to think practically and plan
strategically about what could be possible in political endeavors.
Secondly, Ann Richards consistently pushed me out of my com-
fort zone and gave me countless opportunities to learn, be involved, and serve causes that mattered to me. My friend Ernesto
Cortes taught me to look at politics and governing with the eyes
of a grandmother in order to focus beyond immediate goals and
imagine the consequences of political actions on future generations. When my granddaughters Lauren and Lindsey came along,
I finally understood what he meant. Jack Martin, one of the wise
sages in business and politics, has been my friend and sounding
board for more than 30 years, helping me to stay anchored in political realities.

Over the years, I've made many enduring friendships through Democratic politics in what is now a solidly Republican state. With all of my speculations about our future, I hope that I don't embarrass those friends with my current follies. I speak for myself, and not for them.

When I decided I wanted to write about some of my amorphous political experiences, my agent, Jim Hornfischer, pushed and prodded until I could come up with a coherent theme that might serve as a framework for a book. I am grateful for his ideas and continued support. At St. Martin's Press, my editor, Elisabeth Dyssegaard, kept me focused on the stories that could drive a narrative and her gentle comments along the way provided the guidance I needed. Donna Cherry kept me on schedule (mostly!), and Sarah Hanson's copyediting saved me from embarrassment. Michael Cantwell's review was invaluable.

I am grateful to both Republicans and Democrats who were willing to talk to me about their political experiences and how they viewed recent changes in Texas. Among the most notable were former assistant secretary of the U.S. Department of Education, Tom Luce; former U.S. senator Kay Bailey Hutchison; Congressman Joaquin Castro; plus several state legislators, including Jason Villalba, Richard Raymond, Chris Turner, and others. I am particularly indebted to Pat Pangburn, Lisa Turner, Matt Angle, and Russell Langley, who guided me through the morass of Dallas politics. Political scientist Dr. Cal Jillson, who has written extensively about Texas policy and politics, provided valuable insight about what came to be known as the "Texas Way." Dr. James Henson, who heads the Texas Politics Project at the University of Texas at Austin, and Dr. Richard Murray, director of the Survey Research

Institute at the University of Houston, helped me understand recent political trends. Sr. Christine Stevens, Josephine Lopez Paul, and Jacob Cortes helped me understand what is happening in the diverse Hispanic communities they serve, as well as the changes under way in the Catholic Church under Pope Francis.

My dear friends—and ace editors—Mary Mapes and Betty Sue Flowers took the time to read the manuscript in its early rough form, and their comments were enormously helpful. My son, Billy Rogers, who has a political consulting firm based in Nevada and has a knack for analytics, helped me understand the "numbers" required to win political campaigns. (If mistakes are found in my numbers analysis, they are mine, not his.) Many veterans of political campaigns provided valuable "inside" information that I could not have found elsewhere. They include James Aldrete, Cathy Bonner, Chad Clanton, Susan Criss, Matthew Dowd, Patsy Martin, Jeff Rotkoff, George Shipley, Glenn Smith, and others who labored in the 2014 Texas campaigns and spoke to me on the condition of anonymity. My wonderful siblings—Martha Coniglio, Susie Calmes, and Frank Coniglio, as well as my nephew Anthony Coniglio—reviewed parts of the manuscript with grace and humor—and a lot of suggestions! Finally, a word of deepest gratitude to my daughter, Eleanor Petterson, and my son, Billy Rogers, whose love and support sustain me every day, and to whom this book is dedicated.

In looking back on a lifetime in politics, I remember what my friend and co-worker Don Temples once said about our exciting, demanding days working for Ann Richards, who had given us a chance to influence public policy, meet fascinating leaders, and make a difference in the lives of people in our state. When we were packing up Ann's papers and getting ready to move out of the governor's office after her defeat in 1994, Don reminisced about our time there. "Who would have thought," he said, "that ordinary people like us could ever have had such extraordinary experiences in a state like Texas?" He was right. We were just ordinary folks with big dreams. For all of the experiences and cherished friendships from those days, I am eternally grateful.

Notes

Introduction: Why It Matters

1. The Texans who funded the "Swift Boat" campaign included Houston home-builder Bob Perry, $4.45 million; Dallas waste-management magnate Harold Simmons, $3 million; oil tycoon T. Boone Pickens Jr., $2 million; and George W. Bush's top five fundraisers, who jointly put another $1 million into the effort.
2. Grover Norquist, "Defunding the Democratic Party," *The American Spectator*, June 2014.
3. Robert Bartlett Haas, ed., *How Writing Is Written: Volume II of the Previously Uncollected Writings of Gertrude Stein* (Santa Barbara, CA: Black Sparrow Press, 1977).
4. "Yellow Dog Democrat" is a political term generally applied to any Democratic Party loyalist who would vote for a Democrat over a Republican under any condition. The term originated after the Civil War, when the Republican Party was anathema to Southern Democrats who often declared that they would rather vote for a yellow dog than a Republican. By the 1940s and '50s, New Deal Democrats, generally liberal and loyal to their national party, began using the term in a different context than it had been used in the post–Civil War era.

Chapter One: Reality of Defeat–One More Time

1. Pat Pangburn, interview by author, April 27, 2015.
2. Molly Redden, "The Wealthy Woman Behind Wendy Davis," *The New Republic*, July 8, 2013, www.newrepublic.com/article/112760/meet-amber-mostyn -wendy-daviss-most-powerful-political-patron.
3. Ibid.
4. Elizabeth McKenna and Hahrie Han, *Groundbreakers: How Obama's 2.2 Million Volunteers Transformed Campaigning in America* (New York: Oxford University Press, 2014), 96.
5. Wayne Slater, "As Wendy Davis Touts Life Story in Race for Governor, Key Facts Blurred," *The Dallas Morning News*, January 18, 2014, http://www

.dallasnews.com/news/politics/headlines/20140118-as-wendy-davis-touts
-life-story-in-race-for-governor-key-facts-blurred.ece.

6. The author had several conversations over dinner with Karin Johanson during her stay in Texas. Some of the information about the campaign came from these meetings. Most of the information about the internal workings of the campaign came from various members of the staff at both high and low levels. All declined to go on the record.

7. Chris Turner, interview by author, January 8, 2015.

Chapter Two: Lessons of 2014

1. Exiting polling actually showed that the 2014 white voter turnout was about 65 percent. Lincoln Park Strategies, a research and data modeling firm in Washington D.C., reports that although the percentage of white voters is gradually declining in Texas as the percentage of eligible Hispanic voters increases, it still remains in the 63 to 67 percent range in certain elections. See Lincoln Park Strategies, www.LPSStrategies.com.

2. David Stebenne, "How Obama Won Ohio, an Ohio Historian Saw Union Organizers Keeping and Turning Out Voters," *Alternet*, November 7, 2012, www.alternet.org/how-obama-won-office.

3. Elizabeth McKenna and Hahrie Han, *Groundbreakers: How Obama's 2.2 Million Volunteers Transformed Campaigning in America* (New York: Oxford University Press, 2014), 96.

4. Dave Carney, "Battleground Texas' Bleak Future," *Trib Talks, The Texas Tribune*, April 8, 2015. Carney is a noted Republican consultant who worked for former Texas governor Rick Perry, as well as for Greg Abbott, who defeated Wendy Davis in 2014.

5. Dr. Richard Murray, interview by author, February 3, 2015.

6. Chris Turner, interview by author, January 8, 2015.

7. J. David McSwane and Jonathan Tilove, "How Battleground Texas Hobbled the Wendy Davis Campaign," *Austin American-Statesman*, November 8, 2014; Reeve Hamilton, "What Went Wrong with Battleground Texas?" *The Texas Tribune*, November 5, 2014; Robert Draper, "The Future of Battleground Texas . . . Does It Have a Future?, *Texas Monthly*, February 26, 2015; Christopher Hooks, "Losing Ground," *The Texas Observer*, December 30, 2014.

8. Susan Criss, interview by author, April 7, 2015.

9. Jeremy Bird, interview by author, February 26, 2015. All other Jeremy Bird quotations in this book are from this interview unless otherwise noted.

Chapter Three: Rise of the Outsiders

1. Tom Luce, interview by author, January 29, 2015. All other Luce quotations in the book are from this interview unless otherwise noted.

2. For a realistic rendering of the lives of Texas's early wealthy ranchers, see Francis Vick and Jane Monday, *Letters to Alice, Birth of the Kleberg-King Ranch Dynasty* (College Station: Texas A&M University Press, 2012).

3. Cal Jillson, *Lone Star Tarnished: A Critical Look at Texas Politics and Public Policy* (New York: Routledge, 2015), 41.
4. Ibid., 23, 27.
5. For a better understanding of how ordinary people identify with those who rule them, see Corey Robin, *The Reactionary Mind, Conservatism from Edmund Burke to Sarah Palin* (New York: Oxford University Press, 2011), 35.
6. Businessman and philanthropist Andrew Carnegie donated money to small towns and rural communities all over the United States to create lending libraries. More than 2,500 were built between 1883 and 1929. Local communities usually requested these grants.
7. Jillson, *Lone Star Tarnished,* 22.
8. "Mongrelization" was the loathsome term often used by racists and arch-segregationist politicians to decry any attempt to integrate or "mix" the races in schools, public facilities, the military, or any other activity because it might lead to intermarriages that would produce mix-raced children—thus destroying the "purity" of the white race. As a child growing up in Texas, I heard public officials use this term repeatedly. It finally disappeared from polite conversation in the 1960s.
9. In *Means of Ascent,* the second in his four-book chronicle of Lyndon Johnson, biographer Robert Caro comes close to proving that Johnson stole the election. But old-time Johnson loyalists dispute the claim and counter that no one actually knows what really happened in that election because there was so much voter fraud all around.
10. David Richards, *Once Upon a Time in Texas: A Liberal in the Lone Star State* (Austin: University of Texas Press, 2002), 10.
11. The "Johnson boys" included John Connally, who would be elected governor of Texas as a Democrat before he became a Nixon Republican; Robert Strauss, who would head the national Democratic Party before becoming U.S. trade representative and one of the most powerful men in Washington; Lloyd M. Bentsen Jr., who would serve in the U.S. Senate and as secretary of the Treasury under President Bill Clinton. Others in Johnson's inner circle went on to become members of Congress, run the powerful University of Texas system, or head the state's major law firms and many of its largest philanthropies. Their influence is still felt in pockets of politics today.

Chapter Four: Blame It on Perot—and on Liberals, Too

1. Nationally, Perot gained about 19 percent of the popular vote, but failed to win the electoral vote of any state. In Texas, he got 22 percent of the vote to Bush's 40.5 percent and Clinton's 37 percent.
2. Robert Noyce made an almost simultaneous discovery of a microchip circuit in California and became one of the founders of the Intel Corporation. Kilby and Noyce were considered co-inventors of the integrated circuit. When Kilby accepted the Nobel Prize in 2000, he gave full credit to Noyce, who had died in 1990. Kilby also developed the first handheld calculator, which would make a fortune for his employer, Texas Instruments.

3. Daniel Hartley, "Urban Decline in Rust Belt Cities," *Federal Reserve Bank of Cleveland Economic Commentary,* Number 2013-06, May 20, 2013.

4. Texas State Historical Association, "Collin County Facts," *Handbook of Texas Online,* tshaonline.org.

5. Sean P. Cunningham, *Cowboy Conservatism: Texas and the Rise of the Modern Right* (Lexington: University of Kentucky Press, 2010), 212.

6. Population data comes from "Census and Census Reports," *Handbook of Texas Online,* June 12, 2010, tshaonline.org.

7. David Richards, *Once Upon a Time in Texas: A Liberal in the Lone Star State* (Austin: University of Texas Press, 2002), 10.

8. Ibid., 52–56.

9. Robert Bryce, *Cronies: How Texas Business Became American Policy and Brought Bush to Power* (New York: PublicAffairs, 2004), 96-97.

10. In 1971 and 1972, one of the biggest public corruption episodes to occur in Texas political history sent a number of high-ranking Democrats to jail and destroyed the careers of a dozen others. Houston banker Frank Sharp gave almost $1 million in loans to numerous state officials in a scheme to generate profits for his banks and other companies. The Democratic Speaker of the house went to prison, as did the state insurance commissioner and others. Texas liberals were able to win a number of legislative races because so many conservative Democrats were implicated in the scandal.

11. Ann Richards's core group of female friends who played an important role in her career, and in her gubernatorial administration, included lawyers Jane Hickie, Martha Smiley, Sarah Weddington, Claire Korioth, and Judith Guthrie; entrepreneurs Cathy Bonner and Katherine (Chula) Reynolds; writer Liz Carpenter; publisher Ellen Temple; professor and primary speechwriter Suzanne Coleman; ERA leader Barbara Vackar; and close friends who preceded her in death: Virginia Whitten, Pat Cole, and Nancy Kohler. Beyond this inner circle, there were at least a dozen other women who were close to Richards and important to her career, the development of the Texas women's movement, and the building of a progressive movement for Democrats from the 1970s to the 1990s.

12. Wayne Thorburn, *Red State: An Insider's Story of How the GOP Came to Dominate Texas Politics* (Austin: University of Texas Press, 2014), 107.

Chapter Five: Permanent Breakthrough

1. Robert Bryce, *Cronies: How Texas Business Became American Policy and Brought Bush to Power* (New York: PublicAffairs, 2004), 83.

2. Carolyn Barta, *Bill Clements: Texian to his Toenails* (Austin: Eakin Press, 1996), 180–90.

3. Ibid., 211.

4. Sean P. Cunningham, *Cowboy Conservatism: Texas and the Rise of the Modern Right* (Lexington: University of Kentucky Press, 2010), 192.

5. Barta, *Bill Clements,* 211.

6. Jack Martin, interview by author, April 22, 2015. All subsequent quotes by Martin are from this interview, unless otherwise indicated.

7. Barta, *Bill Clements,* 214.
8. Ibid., 217.
9. Ibid., 228.
10. Wayne Thorburn, *Red State: An Insider's Story of How the GOP Came to Dominate Texas Politics* (Austin: University of Texas Press, 2014), 104-105. Thorburn's book details the demographic and voting trends that clearly demonstrate the reach of Republicans and their rise to power.
11. Cunningham, *Cowboy Conservatism,* 227.
12. Karl Rove, *Courage and Consequence: My Life as a Conservative in the Fights* (New York: Simon & Schuster, 2010), 55.
13. Cunningham, *Cowboy Conservatism,* 238.
14. Thorburn, *Red State,* 133.
15. Ibid., 191.
16. After consulting in numerous political campaigns, Jack Martin in 1988 founded Public Strategies, a unique national business-consulting firm that pioneered a new model in business communications, as well as brand and investor relations strategies. He consulted for some of the world's largest corporations. His firm was acquired by the London-based conglomerate WPP in 2006, and Martin became global executive chairman and CEO of Hill + Knowlton Strategies, whose clients included over half of the Fortune Global 500 list. Martin remained a close friend of Texas governor Ann Richards, who later went to work for his firm. He has also served as a senior advisor to the Democratic National Committee and the U.S. Senate Democratic Committee.
17. Matthew Dowd, interview by author, February 5, 2015.
18. Richard Murray, interview by author, February 3, 2015.

Chapter Six: The Illusion of Victory

1. The 1990 campaign staff included Ann's close friends Jane Hickie and Cathy Bonner, as well as her key press aide Bill Cryer, who left his state job to work on the campaign. Also included were Richard Moya, Carl Ritchie, Joy Anderson, Billy Ramsey, Fred Ellis, Monte Williams, Chuck McDonald, Margaret Justice, Paul Williams, Juan Barrientos, Celia Israel, Glenn Maxey, Claire Korioth, Katherine "Chula" Reynolds, and too many more to name. They provided daily efforts at state and local headquarters in every area of the state to bring about the unprecedented victory of Ann Richards, the first female governor of Texas to win in her own right. It was such a bonding experience that most of us have remained friends for life.
2. Reinhold Niebuhr, *The Children of Light and the Children of Darkness* (New York: Charles Scribner's Sons, 1960), 41.
3. The exact quote is from Matthew 10:16: "Behold I send you out as sheep in the midst of wolves; so be wise as serpents and innocent as doves." *The New Oxford Annotated Bible, Revised Standard Version* (New York: Oxford University Press, 1971).
4. *The Red Shoes* (1948), directed by Michael Powell and Emeric Pressburger, was a critically acclaimed film, loosely based on a fairy tale by Hans Christian Andersen.

5. Jack Martin and I, along with Richards's then chief of staff John Fainter, had a similar conversation with her later on. In it, she said that one reason she had to run for reelection was that she didn't see another Democrat on the horizon at the time who could win the race. By this time, I had already left the governor's office to teach at the Lyndon B. Johnson School of Public Affairs at the University of Texas at Austin. I left the teaching post to run her reelection campaign.

6. Karl Rove, *Courage and Consequence: My Life as a Conservative in the Fight* (New York: Simon & Schuster, 2010), 92.

7. Ibid., 84.

8. Of the original "Gang of Four," three were no longer on the political scene in 1998. Former attorney general Jim Mattox had lost his Democratic primary race for governor to Ann Richards in 1990; Republican Rick Perry had defeated Agriculture Commissioner Jim Hightower in 1990; and of course former state treasurer and governor Ann Richards lost her reelection bid in 1994.

Chapter Seven: Clowns, Crackpots, and Christian Crusaders

1. Jay Root, Ross Ramsey and Jim Rutenberg, "For Perry, Lobbyist Is a Take No Prisoners Ally," *New York Times,* October 14, 2011, http://www.nytimes.com/2011/10/15/us/politics/mike-toomey-texas-lobbyist-is-power-behind-perry.html?_r=0.

2. Ibid.

3. Ibid.

4. Before the advent of modern computer technology, accountants and bank clerks handled all check processing, ledgers, etc. by hand. Because the work was so detailed, most wore green eyeshades to shut out the harsh lighting then in use that might cause a glare. The green eye-shade days also existed in the newspaper industry—particularly with copy editors on news desks. The term "green eye shade" became associated with tedious deskwork in the early twentieth century. When Ann Richards became treasurer, almost all of the sorting of checks and accounting functions had never been transferred to computer technology, which was widely available in the banking industry.

5. Cal Jillson, *Lone Star Tarnished: A Critical Look at Texas Politics and Public Policy* (New York: Routledge, 2014), 50.

6. Ibid.

7. Ibid., 51.

8. Ibid., 17.

9. Ezra Klein, "Obama Derangement Syndrome," *Vox,* February 23, 2014, http://www.vox.com/2015/2/23/8089639/obama-derangement-syndrome.

10. Kay Bailey Hutchison, interview by author, February 25, 2015.

11. Wayne Thorburn, *Red State: An Insider's Story of How the GOP Came to Dominate Texas Politics* (Austin: University of Texas Press, 2014), 142.

12. John H. Fund, "Betting on Rick Perry," *American Spectator,* October 2011.

13. James C. McKinley Jr. and Clifford Krauss, "'Yes' for Texas Governor Is 'No' to Washington," *New York Times,* March 2, 2010, http://nytimes.com/i2010/0303/us//03texas.html.

14. Tom Benning, "Supporters, Opponents of Gay Marriage Press Their Case at Texas Capitol," *Trail Blazers Blog, Dallas Morning News,* March 24, 2015, http://trailblazersblog.dallasnews.com/2015/03/supporters-opponents-of-gay-marriage-press-their-case-at-texas-capital.html/.
15. Sandhya Somashekhar, "Texas Attorney General Defiant over Court's Same-Sex Marriage Decision," *Washington Post,* June 28, 2015, http://www.washingtonpost.com/national/texas-attorney-general-defiant-over-courts-same-sex-marriage-decision/2015/06/28/16faa160-1dcf-11e5-84d5-eb37ee8eaa61_story.html.
16. Enrique Rangel, "State Officials Blast Supreme Court Ruling," *Amarillo Globe News,* July 26, 2015, http://amarillo.com/news/local-news/2015-06-26/couples-state-officials-react-same-sex-marriage-ruling.
17. Richard Parker, "Giving the Boot to Local Control," *Dallas Morning News,* March 18, 2015, http://www.dallasnews.com/opinion/latest-columns/201503 17-richard-parker-welcome-to-the-era-of-the-big-governmet-republican.ece.
18. Forest Wilder, "The Money Behind Texas' Most Influential Think Tank," *Texas Observer,* January 6, 2014, http://www.texasobserver.org/money-behind-texas-public-policy-foundation.
19. Ibid.
20. Aman Batheja and Julian Aguilar, "Straus Says House Will Stand Up to Bullies," *Texas Tribune,* February 11, 2015, http://www.texastribune.org/2015/02/11/straus-texas-house-members-arent-going-to-be-bullied.
21. Peter Wehner, "Conservatives in Name Only," *New York Times,* January 15, 2015, http://www.nytimes.com/2015/01/15/opinion/conservatives-in-name-only.html.
22. Attorney General Ken Paxton was indicted by the Collin County grand jury on January 31, 2015, on two counts of first-degree securities fraud and one count of third-degree failure to register as a securities agent. The Texas Rangers led the investigation that led to the indictments. Paxton has vowed to fight the charges.
23. Jennifer Bendery, "Louie Gohmert: Aurora Shootings Result of 'Ongoing Attacks on Judeo-Christian Beliefs,'" *Huffington Post,* July 20, 2012, http://www.huffingtonpost.com . . . /louie-gohmert-aurora-shootings_n_1689099.html.
24. "Quote to Note," *Texas Tribune,* October 1, 2014, http://www.texastribune.org/2i014/10/01/brief/.
25. Andrew Schneider, "In Houston, Falling Oil Prices Spark Fears of Job Cuts Beyond Energy," NPR, March 3, 2015, www.npr.org/2015/03/03/390159176/in-houston-falling-oil-prices-spark-fears-of-job-cuts-beyond-energy.
26. Most states have some sort of severance tax, also known as a gross production tax, on the extraction of nonrenewable natural resources—oil, gas, timber, uranium, or other materials—usually a percentage of the market value of the product. Numerous exemptions and discounts can lower the cost of production taxes.
27. William Rogers, a political consultant based in Nevada, prepared the analysis of oil prices and election results for the author. Rogers also happens to be the author's son.

Chapter Eight: Hispanics–Hype and Hope

1. Corrie MacLaggan, "Report: Texas Lags In Hispanic Voter Turnout," *Texas Tribune*, February 26, 2014, www.texastribune.org/2014/02/26/Hispanic-voters.

2. Gardner Selby, "Karl Rove Says Republicans Running in Texas Draw 40 Percent of Latino Vote on Average," PolitiFact.com, June 4, 2013, wwww.politifact.com /texas . . . /karl-rove/karl-rove-says-republicans-running-texas-draw-49-p/.

3. Wayne Thorburn, *Red State: An Insider's Story of How the GOP Came to Dominate Texas Politics* (Austin: University of Texas Press, 2014), 219, citing a Reuters/IPSOS exit poll published March 6, 2013, indicating that 27.2 percent of Texas Hispanic voters self-identified as Republican.

4. Quoted in Thorburn, *Red State*, 221, from Melody C. Mendoza, "Experts Discuss Latino Vote, Impact on Texas," *San Antonio Express-News*, December 9, 2012.

5. James Aldrete, interview by author, April 24, 2015.

6. Sierra Stoney and Jeanne Batalova, "Spotlight: Central American Immigrants in the United States," Migration Policy Institute, March 18, 2013.

7. Richard Peña Raymond, interview by author, February 4, 2015.

8. "The Cisneros Probe: Key Stories," *Washington Post*, http://www.washington post.com/wp-srv/politics/special/cisneros/keystories.htm.

9. Eric Hananoki, "The Libre Initiative: A Koch-Funded Group Being Passed Off as Empowering Hispanics," *Media Matters for America*, March 2, 2015, www.mediamatters.org/blog/2015/03/02/the-libre-initiative-a-koch-funded -group-being/202450.

10. Ibid.

11. Ibid.

12. Ibid. The *Media Matters* article also quoted two different segments on Fox News that referred to Libre Initiative as the voice of the Hispanic Community: one featured *Fox and Friends* co-host Gretchen Carlson interviewing a representative of Libre Initiative that aired July 12, 2013; the other was *America's News HQ* with reporter Peter Doocy, which aired December 10, 2013.

13. Zac Drain, "Is Jason Villalba the Future of the Texas GOP?" *D Magazine*, October 2012, www.dmagazine.com/publications/d-magazine/2012/October /is-jason-villalba-the-future-of-the-texas-gop.

14. State Representative Jason Villalba, interview by author, February 20, 2015. Unless otherwise noted, all quotations from Villalba are from this interview.

15. Elizabeth Dias, "Why One in Four U.S. Latinos Now Identify as Former Catholics," *Time*, May 7, 2014, http://time.com/89646/why-one-in-four-u-s -latinos-now-identify-as-former-catholics/.

16. "The Shifting Religious Identity of Latinos in the United States," Pew Research Center, May 7, 2014, http://www.pewforum.org/2014/05/07/the -shifting-religious-identity-of-latinos-in-the-united-states.

17. Josh Baugh, "From Political Matriarch Rosie Castro, the Sons Also Rise," *San Antonio Express-News*, September 29, 2012, http://www.mysanantonio.com /news/loc-political-matriarch-the-sons-also-rise-3905913.

18. Herschel "Herky" Bernard's son Jeremy became the first male social secretary to serve in the White House when President Obama appointed him to that position in 2011. Participants in those Karam's luncheons in the 1960s left a significant political legacy in Texas and in national political life.
19. Baugh, "From Political Matriarch Rosie Castro, the Sons Also Rise."
20. Andy Kroll, "The Power of Two," *National Journal,* January 24, 2015, http://www.nationaljournal.com/magazine/the-power-of-two-20150123.
21. Ibid.
22. Congressman Joaquin Castro, interview by author, May 15, 2015. Unless otherwise noted, all other quotations from Castro are from this interview.
23. Kroll, "The Power of Two."
24. Joaquin Castro, "Mr. Castro Goes to Washington," *Texas Monthly,* February 2014, http://www.texasmonthly.com/story/behind-the-scenes-of-joaquin-castros-first-year-in-congress?fullpage=1.
25. Kroll, "The Power of Two."

Chapter Nine: A New Texas Way

1. William H. Frey, *Diversity Explosion: How New Racial Demographics Are Remaking America* (Washington, D.C.: Brookings Institution Press, 2015). Frey's analysis of the movement of minorities to American suburbs is the most comprehensive study of the internal migration that is changing the compositions of cities, suburbs, and states across the country.
2. Coral Davenport and Laurie Goodstein, "Pope's Climate Plan Vexes Right," *New York Times,* April 28, 2015, http://www.nytimes.com/2015/04/28/world/Europe/pope-francis-steps-up-campaign-on-climate-change-to-conservatives-alarm.html.
3. Ibid.
4. Amy Davidson, "God and the GOP," *New Yorker,* February 9, 2015, http://www.newyorker/magazine/2015/02/09/god-g-o-p.
5. Mary Wisniewski, "Most Catholics Vote for Obama, but Latinos and Whites Divided," Reuters, November 8, 2012, mobile.reuters.com/article/idUSBRE8A71M420121108.
6. Josephine Lopez Paul, interview by author, February 13, 2015.
7. "Francis on 'The Joy of the Gospel," *America: The National Catholic Review,* November 26, 2013, http://www.americamagazine.org/issue/francis-on-the-joy-of-the-gospel.
8. I am a member of the board of the nonprofit Interfaith Education Fund, which provides education and training for members of these local community organizations involved in long-term relationship building to empower citizens to take direct action on key issues in their areas. In 1990, I published a book about the work of these organizations, and their leader, Ernesto Cortes. See Mary Beth Rogers, *Cold Anger: A Story of Faith and Power Politics* (Denton: University of North Texas Press, 1990).
9. Jacob Cortes, interview by author, February 25, 2015.
10. Although the Texas bill HB1403 became a model for more than a dozen states that later enacted similar legislation to allow the children of undocumented

immigrants to take advantage of the lower college tuition costs provided to state residents, it was not referred to in Texas as the Dream Act until after similar federal legislation was introduced with bipartisan support in 2011. Since then, the in-state tuition program is commonly known as the Texas Dream Act. The acronym DREAM comes from the official title of the proposed federal legislation, the Development, Relief and Education for Alien Minors Act.

11. Jens Manuel Krogstad and Jeffrey S. Passel, "5 Facts About Illegal Immigration in the U.S.," Pew Research Center, November 18, 2014, http://www.pew research.org/fact-tank/2014/11/18.

12. David Edwards, "Louie Gohmert Demands Obama Stop 'Luring' Lice and Scabies-Ridden Immigrant Children," *Raw Story*, June 26, 2014, http://www .rawstory.com/2014/06/louie-gohmert-demands-obama-stop-luring-lice-and -scabies-ridden-immigrant-children.

13. Esther Yu-His Lee, "Congressman Goes on Diatribe Against Migrant Children, Urges Texas to Unilaterally Declare War," ThinkProgress.org, July 11, 2014, http://thinkprogress.org/immigration/2014/07/11/3459331/gohmert -unaccompanied-children-dd.

14. W. Gardner Selby, "Immigrants Bring 'Third-World Diseases,'" PolitiFact .com, June 20, 2014, http://www.politifact.com/texas/statements/2014/jun/20 /battleground-texas/dan-patrick-has-called-illegal-immigration-invasio/.

15. John Savage, "Advocates Rally in Support of Texas DREAM Act," *Texas Observer*, January 14, 2015, http://www.texasobserver.org/advocates-rally-support -texas-dream-act.

16. Dianne Solís, "Dallas Latinos Savor Legislative Win on In-State Tuition for Immigrants," *Dallas Morning News*, June 2, 2015, http://www.dallasnews.com /news/metro/20150602-latinos-savor-legislative-win-on-in-state-tuition-for -migrants.ece.

17. Zoltan L. Hajnal, "Opposition to Immigration Reform Is a Winning Strategy for Republicans," *Monkey Cage* (blog), *Washington Post*, February 27, 2014, http://www.washingtonpost.com/bogs/monkey-cage/wp/2014/02/27 /opposition-to-immigration-reform-is-a-winning-strategy-for-republicans.

18. Terrence Stutz and Gromer Jeffers Jr., "For Some Tea Party Leaders, Legislature's Brew Was Weak," *Dallas Morning News*, June 1, 2015, http://www .dallasnews.com/news/politics/state-politics/20150601-for-some-tea-party -leaders-legislatures-brew-was-weak.ece.

19. Brandi Grissom, "Republicans Keep Quiet Following Paxton Indictment," *Dallas Morning News*, August 2, 2015, http://www.dallasnews.com/news/local -news/20150801-republicans-keep-quiet-following-paxton-indictment.ece.

20. Christy Hoppe, "Amid Conspiracy Talk, Abbott Orders Texas Guard to Keep an Eye on Federal Military Training," *Dallas Morning News*, April 28, 2015, http://www.dallasnews.com/news/politics/headlines/20150428-abbott-orders -federal-military-training-in-texas-watched-amid-conspiracy-talk.ece.

21. Christy Hoppe, "Ex-GOP Lawmaker Blisters Abbott for 'Pandering to Idiots' over Military Exercise," *The Dallas Morning News*, May 1, 2015, http://www .dallasnews.com/news/politics/headlines/20150430-ex-gop-lawmaker-blis ters-abbott-for-pandering-to-idiots-over-military-exercise.ece.

22. Frey, *Diversity Explosion*, 55.

23. Ibid., 149.
24. Ibid., 140–51.
25. Ibid., 164.
26. Joel B. Pollak, "Blue State Blues: Fleeing Democrats Will Turn Texas Blue," Breitbart.com, March 3, 2014. Pollak's article was based on a research report issued by the Manhattan Institute for Policy Research; Tom Gray and Robert Scardamalia, "The Great California Exodus: A Closer Look," *Civic Report* no. 71 (September 2010), http:/www.manhattan-institute.org/html/cr_71.htm#.Vb97XMZN3zl.
27. Ronald Bronstein, "Bad Bet: Why Republicans Can't Win with Whites Alone," *National Journal*, September 5, 2013, quoted in Frey, *Diversity Explosion*, 225.
28. Richard Dunham, "Demographic Tides May Turn Texas Purple or Blue," *Houston Chronicle*, November 10, 2012.
29. Matt Angle, interview by author, April 29, 2015.
30. Russell Langley, interview by author, April 30, 2015. Ed Ishmael and Tom Solendar were co-founders of TexVAC with Langley.
31. In 2005, Matt Angle created the Lone Star Project, both as a federal PAC and as a Texas general-purpose political action committee. Still in existence, it provides research, candidate recruitment, and strategic coordination with a number of other Texas Democratic groups. In recent years, the Lone Star Project has taken the lead in legal challenges in federal court to halt Texas's discriminatory redistricting plans and restrictive voter registration laws that created barriers to minority voting.
32. Lisa Turner, interview by author, December 30, 2014.

Chapter Ten: Memo to the Future

1. A "Sister Souljah moment" is a political term that refers to some sort of public repudiation of an extreme statement or action within one's own political party. The term originated in 1992, when presidential candidate Bill Clinton denounced the lyrics in a song by hip-hop entertainer Sister Souljah that said, in effect, that there were no good white people. She had also allegedly made a statement that since whites had killed so many black people throughout history, it would be okay for blacks to kill whites. Clinton's rejection of the remarks marked him as a politician who would speak out against all forms of racism and risk offending some African Americans in his own party in order to speak the truth.
2. James Hohmann, "Can Southern Democrats Make a Comeback?" *Politico*, December 5, 2014, http://www.politico.com/story/2014/12/mary-landrieu-democrats-113358.html.
3. Václav Havel, *Living in Truth* (London: Faber and Faber, 1989).
4. Hohmann, "Can Southern Democrats Make a Comeback?"
5. Twyla Tharp, *The Creative Habit* (New York: Simon & Schuster, 2006).
6. Steve H. Murdock and Steve White, Md. Nazrul Hogue, Beverly Pecotta, Xiuhong Yoa, Jennifer Balkan, "A Summary of the Texas Challenge in the Twenty-First Century: Population Change for the Future of Texas," Center for Demographic and Socioeconomic Research and Education, Texas A&M

University, December 2002, http://osd.texas.gov/Resources/Publications/2002
/2002_12_TexasChallengeSummary.pdf. Although it has been 13 years since
this report was issued, the data is still relevant, as the state of Texas has addressed few of the needs detailed in the report. Dr. Murdock is currently director of the Hobby Center for the Study of Texas at Rice University.

7. Karl Rove, *Courage and Consequence: My Life as a Conservative in the Fight* (New
York: Simon & Schuster, 2010), 92.

8. James Henson, interview by author, January 23, 2015.

Afterword

1. Michael P. McDonald, "General Election Turnout," United States Elections
Project, December 30, 2014, http://www.electproject.org/home/voter-turnout
/voter-turnout-data/2014g.

2. Mary Beth Rogers, *Barbara Jordan: American Hero* (New York: Bantam Books,
1998), 341.

3. Elisabeth Young-Bruehl, "Reading Hannah Arendt's *The Life of the Mind*,"
in Elisabeth Young-Bruehl, *Mind and the Body Politic* (New York: Routledge,
1989), 25.

4. Some of these questions have been used by educator Deborah Meier to teach
elementary school children habits of critical thinking and are explained in her
book *The Power of Their Ideas* (Boston: Beacon Press, 1995, 2002).

5. Nikos Kazantzakis, *The Saviors of God: Spiritual Exercises* (New York: Simon &
Schuster, 1960).

Bibliography

Catholic News Service. "Francis on 'The Joy of the Gospel." *America: The National Catholic Review,* November 26, 2013.

Baker, Russ. *Family of Secrets: The Bush Dynasty, America's Invisible Government, and the Hidden History of the Last Fifty Years.* New York: Bloomsbury, 2009.

Barta, Carolyn. *Bill Clements: Texian to his Toenails.* Austin: Eakin Press, 1996.

Baugh, Josh. "From Political Matriarch Rosie Castro, the Sons Also Rise." *San Antonio Express-News,* September 29, 2012.

Bendery, Jennifer. "Louie Gohmert: Aurora Shootings Result of 'Ongoing Attacks on Judeo-Christian Beliefs.'" *Huffington Post,* July 20, 2013.

Benning, Tom. "Supporters, Opponents of Gay Marriage Press Their Case at Texas Capitol." *Dallas Morning News,* March 23, 2015.

Bennis, Warren. *Why Leaders Can't Lead: The Unconscious Conspiracy Continues.* San Francisco: Jossey-Bass, 1991.

Batheja, Aman, and Julián Aguilar. "Straus Says House Will Stand Up to Bullies." *Texas Tribune,* February 11, 2015.

Bryce, Robert. *Cronies: How Texas Business Became American Policy—And Brought Bush to Power.* New York: PublicAffairs, 2004.

Carney, Dave."Battleground Texas' Bleak Future." *Trib Talks* (blog), *Texas Tribune,* April 8, 2015.

Castro, Joaquin. "Mr. Castro Goes to Washington." *Texas Monthly,* February 2014.

Cunningham, Sean P. *Cowboy Conservatism: Texas and the Rise of the Modern Right.* Lexington: University Press of Kentucky, 2010.

Davenport, Coral, and Laurie Goodstein. "Pope's Climate Plan Vexes Right." *New York Times,* April 28, 2015.

Davidson, Amy. "Comment: God and the GOP." *New Yorker,* February 9, 2015.

Dias, Elizabeth. "Why One in Four U.S. Latinos Now Identify as Former Catholics." *Time,* May 7, 2014.

Drain, Zac. "Is Jason Villalba the Future of the Texas GOP?" *D Magazine,* October 2012.

Draper, Robert. "The Future of Battleground Texas . . . Does It Have a Future? *Texas Monthly,* February 26, 2014.

Dubose, Lou, and Jan Reid. *The Hammer Comes Down: The Nasty, Brutish and Shortened Political Life of Tom DeLay.* New York: PublicAffairs, 2004.

Dunham, Richard. "Demographic Tides May Turn Texas Purple Or Blue." *Houston Chronicle,* November 10, 2012.

Edwards, David. "Louie Gohmert Demands Obama Stop 'Luring' Lice and Scabies-Ridden Immigrant Children." *Raw Story,* June 26, 2014.

Frey, William H. *Diversity Explosion: How New Racial Demographics Are Remaking America.* Washington, DC: Brookings Institution Press, 2015.

Fund, John H. "Betting on Rick Perry." *American Spectator,* October 2011.

Gray, Tom, and Robert Scardamalia. "The Great California Exodus: A Closer Look," *Civic Report* no 71 (September 2010).

Grieder, Erica. *Big, Hot, Cheap, and Right: What America Can Learn from the Strange Genius of Texas.* New York: PublicAffairs, 2013.

Grissom, Brandi. "Paxton Indicted, Democrats, Watch Dog Groups Scold as State GOP Keeps Quiet." *Dallas Morning News,* August 2, 2015.

Haas, Robert Bartlett, ed. *How Writing Is Written: Volume II of the Previously Uncollected Writings of Gertrude Stein.* Santa Barbara, CA: Black Sparrow Press, 1977.

Hajnal, Zoltan L. "Opposition to Immigration Reform Is a Winning Strategy for Republicans," *Monkey Cage* (blog), *Washington Post,* February 27, 2014.

Hamilton, Reeve. "What Went Wrong with Battleground Texas?" *Texas Tribune,* November 5, 2014.

Hananoki, Eric. "The Libre Initiative: A Koch-Funded Group Being Passed Off as Empowering Hispanics." *Media Matters for America,* March 2, 2015.

Handbook of Texas Online. Austin: Texas State Historical Association.

Hartley, Daniel. "Urban Decline in Rust Belt Cities." *Federal Reserve Bank of Cleveland Economic Commentary,* no. 2013–06, May 20, 2013.

Havel, Vàclav. *Living in Truth.* London: Faber and Faber, 1989.

Hohmann, James. "Can Southern Democrats Make a Comeback?" *Politico,* December 5, 2014.

Hooks, Christopher. "Losing Ground." *Texas Observer,* December 30, 2014.

Hoppe, Christy. "Ex-GOP Lawmaker Blisters Abbott for 'Pandering to Idiots' over Military Exercise." *Dallas Morning News,* May 1, 2015.

———. "Abbott Orders Military Training Watched Amid Conspiracy Talk." *Dallas Morning News,* April 29, 2015.

Issenberg, Sasha. *The Victory Lab: The Secret Science of Winning Campaigns.* New York: Broadway Books, 2012.

Jillson, Cal. *Lone Star Tarnished: A Critical Look at Texas Politics and Public Policy.* New York: Routledge, 2014.

Kazantzakis, Nikos. *The Saviors of God: Spiritual Exercises.* New York: Simon & Schuster, 1960.

Klein, Ezra. "Obama Derangement Syndrome." *Vox,* February 23, 2014.

Krogstad, Jens Manuel, and Jeffrey S. Passel. "5 Facts About Illegal Immigration in the US." Pew Research Center, November 18, 2014.

Kroll, Andy. "The Power of Two." *National Journal,* January 24, 2015.

MacLaggan, Corrie. "Report: Texas Lags in Hispanic Voter Turnout." *Texas Tribune,* February 26, 2014.

McDonald, Michael P. "General Election Turnout." United States Elections Project, December 30, 2014.

McKenna, Elizabeth, and Hahrie Han. *Groundbreakers: How Obama's 2.2 Million Volunteers Transformed Campaigning in America.* New York: Oxford University Press, 2014.

McKinley, James C. Jr., and Clifford Krauss. "'Yes' for Texas Governor Is 'No' to Washington." *New York Times,* March 2, 2010.

McSwane, J. David, and Jonathan Tilove. "How Battleground Texas Hobbled the Wendy Davis Campaign." *Austin American-Statesman,* November 8, 2014.

Meier, Deborah. *The Power of Their Ideas.* Boston: Beacon, 1995, 2002.

Miller, Char, ed. *50 Years of* The Texas Observer. San Antonio: Trinity University Press, 2004.

Minutaglio, Bill. *First Son: George W. Bush and the Bush Family Dynasty.* New York: Three Rivers Press, 2001.

Moore, James, and Wayne Slater. *Rove Exposed: How Bush's Brain Fooled America.* Hoboken, NJ: John Wiley & Sons, 2006.

———. *Bush's Brain: How Karl Rove Made George W. Bush Presidential.* Hoboken, NJ: John Wiley & Sons, 2003.

Montejano, David. *Quixote's Soldiers: A Local History of the Chicano Movement, 1966–1981.* Austin: University of Texas Press, 2010.

Murdock, Steve H., and Steve White, Md. Nazrul Hogue, Beverly Pecotte, Xiuhong Yoa, Jennifer Balkan. "A Summary of the Texas Challenge in the Twenty-First Century: Population Change for the Future of Texas." Center for Demographic and Socioeconomic Research and Education, Department of Rural Sociology, Texas A&M University, December 2002.

Niebuhr, Reinhold. *The Children of Light and the Children of Darkness.* New York: Charles Scribner's Sons, 1960.

Norquist, Grover G. "Defunding the Democratic Party." *American Spectator,* June 2014.

Parker, Richard. "Giving the Boot to Local Control." *Dallas Morning News,* March 18, 2015.

Pew Research Center. "The Shifting Religious Identity of Latinos in the United States," May 7, 2014.

Pollak, Joel B. "Blue State Blues: Fleeing Democrats Will Turn Texas Blue." *Breitbart,* March 3, 2014.

Rangel, Enrique. "State Officials Blast Supreme Court Ruling." *Amarillo Globe News,* July 26, 2015.

Ravitch, Diane. *The Death and Life of the Great American School System: How Testing and Choice Are Undermining Education.* New York: Basic Books, 2010.

Redden, Molly. "The Wealthy Woman Behind Wendy Davis." *New Republic,* July 8, 2013.

Richards, David. *Once Upon a Time in Texas: A Liberal in the Lone Star State.* Austin: University of Texas Press, 2002.

Robin, Corey. *The Reactionary Mind: Conservatism from Edmund Burke to Sarah Palin.* New York: Oxford University Press, 2011.

Rogers, Mary Beth. *Barbara Jordan: American Hero.* New York: Bantam, 1998.

Root, Jay, Ross Ramsey, and Jim Rutenberg, "For Perry, Lobbyist Is a Take No Prisoners Ally." *New York Times*, October 14, 2001.

Rove, Karl. *Courage and Consequence: My Life as a Conservative in the Fight*. New York: Simon & Schuster, 2010.

Savage, John. "Advocates Rally in Support of Texas DREAM Act." *Texas Observer*, January 14, 2015.

Schneider, Andrew. "In Houston Falling Oil Prices Spark Fears of Job Cuts Beyond Energy." NPR, March 3, 2015.

Selby, Gardner. "Immigrants Bring 'Third World' Diseases." *PolitiFact*, June 20, 2014.

———. "Karl Rove Says Republicans Running in Texas Draw 40 Percent of Latino Vote on Average." *PolitiFact*, June 4, 2013.

Slater, Wayne. "As Wendy Davis Touts Life Story in Race for Governor, Key Facts Blurred." *Dallas Morning News*, January 18, 2014.

Solís, Dianne. "Dallas Latino Leaders Savor Legislative Win on In-State Tuition for Immigrants." *Dallas Morning News*, June 3, 2015.

Somashekhar, Sandhya. "Texas Attorney General Defiant over Court's Same-Sex Marriage Decision." *Washington Post*, June 28, 2015.

Stoney, Sierra, and Jeanne Batalove. "Spotlight: Central American Immigrants in the United States." Migration Policy Institute, March 18, 2015.

Stutz, Terrence, and Gromer Jeffers Jr. "For Some, Tea Was Too Weak." *Dallas Morning News*, June 2, 2015.

Tharp, Twyla. *The Creative Habit*. New York: Simon & Schuster, 2006.

Thorburn, Wayne. *Red State: An Insider's Story of How the GOP Came to Dominate Texas Politics*. Austin: University of Texas Press, 2014.

Unger, Craig. *Boss Rove: Inside Karl Rove's Secret Kingdom of Power*. New York: Scribner, 2012.

Vick, Francis, and Jane Munday. *Letters to Alice: Birth of the Kleberg-King Ranch Dynasty*. College Station: Texas A&M University Press, 2012.

Vogel, Kenneth P. *Big Money: 2.5 Billion Dollars, One Suspicious Vehicle, and a Pimp—on the Trail of the Ultra-Rich Hijacking American Politics*. New York: PublicAffairs, 2014.

Wehner, Peter. "Conservatives in Name Only." *New York Times*, January 15, 2015.

Wilcox, Clyde, and Carin Robinson. *Onward Christian Soldiers? The Religious Right in American Politics*. Boulder, CO: Westview, 2009.

Wilder, Forrest. "The Money Behind Texas' Most Influential Think Tank." *Texas Observer*, January 6, 2014.

Winegarten, Ruthe Lewin. *Governor Ann Richards & Other Texas Women: From Indians to Astronauts*. Austin: Eakin Press, 1993.

Wisniewski, Mary. "Most Catholics Vote for Obama, but Latinos and Whites Divided." Reuters, November 8, 2012.

Young-Bruehl, Elisabeth. *Mind and the Body Politic*. New York: Routledge, 1989.

Yu-His Lee, Esther. "Congressman Goes on Diatribe Against Migrant Children, Urges Texas to Unilaterally Declare War." ThinkProgress.org, July 11, 2014.

Index

Abbott, Greg, 20–1, 24, 32, 121–3, 132, 138–9, 164, 168–70, 189, 199, 204–5
Aberly, Naomi, 13–15, 208
abortion, 3, 8, 14, 19, 23, 30–2, 70, 77, 90, 92, 114, 117, 124, 129, 161–2, 212
  and pro-choice, 23, 31–2
  and right to life, 3, 8, 19, 77, 124
Adams, Kirk, 89
Afghanistan war, 111
Affordable Care Act, 125, 128–9, 141, 145
African Americans, 21, 27, 32, 36, 45–7, 49, 66, 88–9, 93, 101, 113–15, 124, 151–3, 159, 170–1, 175, 179–82, 187–8, 190, 192–3, 197, 199, 231n1
Aggies for Ann, 177
agrarian populist movement (1870s and '80s), 47
Alamo, 148
Alaniz, Johnny, 151
Aldrete, James, 137
Alger, Bruce, 56
Altria (tobacco), 125
America's Voice, 134
American Dream, 171
American G.I. Forum, 53
American Legislative Exchange Council (ALEC), 125
American Newspaper Guild, 152

Amherst College, 13
"Amway" plan, 34–8
Anchia, Rafael, 150, 166
Angle, Matt, 175–9
anti-Communist hysteria ("Red Scare"), 43–4, 49, 56, 77
Anti–New Deal Democrats ("Texas Regulars"), 49–50
Archer, Christian, 157
Arendt, Hannah, 214
Armey, Dick, 3
Armstrong, Anne, 51, 116
Armstrong, Bob, 70
Armstrong, Joe, 24
Armstrong, Tobin, 51
Asian Americans, 159, 171, 188, 192–3
Astrodome, 104
AT&T, 97
Atlanta, 170–2
Austin, 10, 19, 30, 47, 50, 62, 64, 68–71, 75–6, 82, 87, 100, 109–12, 116, 122, 124, 145, 150, 153, 162, 172, 179, 202–3
Austin, Stephen F., 45
Austin Interfaith, 162
Axelrod, David, 17, 35

Baker, James, 119
Baker Hughes, 130
Baldwin, Tammy, 25
Baron, Fred, 176–7, 180, 182
Barton, Joe, 130

Battle of San Jacinto, 47
Battleground Texas, 7–8, 14–18, 23–7,
  30–41, 182, 201
  as "Battle-Scam," 33
  bifurcation of, 25–6
  post-election analysis of, 37–8
Baylor University, 64, 145
Bell, Cecil, 121
Bell, Chris, 103, 133
Benenson, Joel, 25, 29
Bentsen, Lloyd M., 67, 83–5, 116–17,
  139, 223n11
Bernal, Joe, 66, 151
Bernard, Herschel, 151–2
Bible, 3, 109, 145–6
Bird, Jeremy, 7–8, 15–18, 34–7, 39–40,
  201–2
Blanton, Annie Webb, 48
blogs, 23, 115, 171–2
Blue, Lisa, 177, 182
Bonner, Cathy, 89
Boone, Cecilia, 178
Boone, Garrett, 178
Bowie, James, 148
BP oil spill (2010), 130
Branch, Dan, 127
Brazos County, 173
Bredesen, Phil, 191
Brimer, Kim, 19
Briscoe, Dolph, 75–7, 79
Brown, Jenn, 35, 37
Brownstein, Ronald, 172
Broyles, William, 79
Bush, George H. W., 3, 59, 67, 73–4,
  81–2, 147
Bush, George P., 147–50, 170
Bush, George W., 1–3, 5, 10, 88, 91,
  93–103, 110–11, 115, 119–20,
  132–4, 136, 139, 176, 196, 200–2
  and gubernatorial campaign (1994),
  94–100
  and Hispanic vote, 133–4
  and reelection bid (1998), 100–1
Bush, Jeb, 2, 147, 161
"Bush Derangement Syndrome," 115

C-SPAN, 141

Cabell, Earl, 56
California, 6, 8–9, 77, 109, 135, 171–2,
  207–8, 223n2
"Camp Wannameetagop," 80
Carter, Jimmy, 74, 77, 81
Casey, William J., 171
Castro, Joaquin, 150–1, 153–7
Castro, Julián, 150–1, 153–4, 157
Castro, Maria del Rosario Castro
  ("Rosie"), 150–3
Catholic Church, 31, 138–9, 146–7,
  151, 160–3, 219
  See Pope Francis
CBS, 16
Chavez, Cesar, 68
Cheney, Dick, 119
Chicano movement (1960s), 152–3
Chicano third-party movement (1970s),
  150
"children of darkness," 95
"children of light," 95
Christianity, 3, 9, 41, 82, 105, 107–12,
  123–9, 145–6, 200
  and creationism, 3, 124
  and crusaders, 9, 105, 107–12,
  123–9
  and evangelical movement, 41, 82,
  109, 146–7
  and talk radio, 109, 200
Cisneros, Henry, 140, 153
Citizens United, 5
CityView, 140
Civil Rights Act of 1964, 64
Civil War, 44–5, 62, 113–14
Clements, Bill, 71, 73–83, 85, 100, 107,
  114, 131–2, 189, 202
Clements, Rita Bass, 71, 74, 77–8
climate change, 3, 160–1
Clinton, Bill, 59, 85, 91–2, 100–1, 104,
  116, 140, 190, 223n11
Clinton, Hillary, 15, 85, 187
Coleman, Suzanne, 88–9
College Station, 79
Collin County, 62–3, 173
Collins, James, 84
Colorado, 7–8, 16, 25, 29, 129, 135
Communism, 43–4, 49, 56, 77

Communities Organized for Public Service (COPS), 153–4, 162
Confederate States of America, 45
Connally, John, 76, 89, 223n11
Container Store, 178
"contemporariness," 10
Contract with America, 91
Cornyn, John, 80, 91, 101
Cortes, Ernesto, 153
Cortes, Jacob, 162–3
Craddick, Christi, 204
Criss, Susan, 39
Crude Oil Windfall Profit Tax Act, 81
Cruz, Lauro, 66
Cruz, Ted, 2, 43, 120, 128, 185–6
Cuba, 161
Cuomo, Mario, 91
Czech Republic, 191

Dallas, 8, 13–14, 23, 31, 37, 43–4, 56, 59–69, 73, 75, 81, 84, 100–1, 104, 109, 116, 118, 122, 127, 130, 139, 143–5, 150, 162, 166, 170–83, 203, 218
    as Democratic stronghold, 173–6
    and right-wing activity, 43–4
Dallas Area Interfaith, 162
Dallas County Democratic Party, 177–8
Dallas County Republican Party, 56
Dallas-Fort Worth International Airport, 63
Dallas GOTV program, 179–81
Dallas Morning News, 23–4, 31
Daniel, Price, 54
Daughters of the Republic of Texas, 148
Davis, Wendy, gubernatorial campaign (2014), 8, 13–27, 29–42, 102, 121, 132, 139–40, 182, 187, 189, 198–202, 208
    as "Abortion Barbie," 23, 31
    backlash against, 21–4, 30–1
    and Battleground Texas, 14–18, 23–7, 30–41
    biography of, 18–24, 30–1
    and fame, 22–4
    as feminist, 19, 30–2
    and filibuster, 19–23

and fundraising, 13–27, 198
and lack of preparation, 22–5, 30–1, 198
and lack of strategy, 17–18, 22–7, 30–2, 198
    lessons of, *See* Wendy Davis, lessons of
as marketing commodity, 22–3
and spending, 26–7
and Texas state senate, 19
Davis, Wendy, lessons of, 29–42, 198
    and audience, 31–2
    and control of operations, 32
    and defining message, 32
    and Hispanic voters, 30–2, 36–7
    and plan of action, 30–2
    and strategy, 30–2
    and timing, 30–1
    and volunteer recruitment, 33–8
    and women voters, 30–2
de Santa Anna, General Antonio López, 148
DeLay, Tom ("The Hammer"), 4, 43, 103, 174
Democratic Congressional Campaign Committee (DCCC), 174
Democratic Convention (2012), 154
Democratic National Committee, 15, 177
demographics, 7, 31, 36, 41, 99, 134, 171, 175, 178, 183, 196
    See African Americans; Asian Americans; Hispanics; immigration; minority population; white voters; women
Denton County, 174, 203
Dewhurst, David, 120, 125
direct-mail fund-raising, 82
Dixiecrats, 54
donors, 4–5, 8, 16–17, 24, 29, 34–5, 125, 155–6, 177–8, 182, 199, 215
    See megadonors
Dowd, Matthew, 85, 88, 201
Dr. Pepper Snapple, 61
Dream Act, 163–7
Dugger, Ronnie, 53
Duke University, 117

early voting, 34, 37
Edwards, John, 177
Eisenhower, Dwight D., 51
El Paso, 66, 136
El Salvador, 138
election districts, composition of, 65–6
Electoral College, 6–7, 17, 201
Electronic Data Services (EDS), 59–62
Elementary and Secondary Education
    Act (1965), 108
Ellis, Rodney, 36
Emily's List, 25
Empower Texas, 125
environmental concerns, 3, 160–1,
    193–4, 203–6
  and air and water quality, 213
  and climate change, 3, 160–1
  and fracking, 193, 203–4
  See oil
Equal Rights Amendment (ERA), 70
Erickson, Erick, 23
Ericsson, 61
Ethics and Public Policy Center, 126–7
evangelical movement, 41, 82, 109,
    146–7
  See Christianity
ExxonMobil, 125

Facebook, 20
"fall-off voters," 36
FCC-required conversion to digital
    technology, 112
Federal Reserve Bank of Dallas, 130
feminism, 71, 89–90, 92, 188
filibuster, 8, 14, 19–20, 22, 30
Florida, 6, 16, 187
FOB (friend of Bill Clinton), 100
Ford, Gerald R., 51, 74, 76–7
Fort Hood, 173
Fort Worth, 18, 23–4, 26, 36, 62, 65, 69,
    100, 148–9, 179,
Fox News, 141
fracking, 193, 203–4
free-market ideology, 142, 160
Freedom Partners, 141
FreedomWorks, 4
Frey, William, 171

Friedman, Kinky, 102–3
Frito-Lay, 61
Frost, Martin, 174–6
fundraising, 5, 8, 13–27, 32–3, 82,
    100–1, 157, 208, 212
  See Battleground Texas; megadonors;
    Texas Victory Fund
future for Texas Democrats, 185–216
  and keeping the money in Texas,
    207–9
  and hype, 201–2
  and policies and politics, 203–6,
    211–16
  and Republican extremism, 206–7
  and Republican strategists, 198–201
  and the right leader, 188–91
  and strategy to win, 197–8
  and the white vote, 191–4
  and vision versus message, 194–7
  and whole-state campaigning, 202–3

Gallego, Pete, 149–50
Galveston, 16, 39
gang of four, 83–6, 100, 206n8
Garcia, Sylvia R., 150
Garza, Daniel, 141
gay rights, 88–9, 93–4, 121–2, 124,
    129–30, 146, 160–1, 166–7, 172,
    174–5, 197, 200
General Motors, 64–5
GEO Group, 125
George R. Brown Convention Center,
    104
get-out-the-vote (GOTV), 16, 27,
    33–5, 78, 81, 84, 136, 138, 179–82,
    187
Giddings, Helen, 179
Gingrich, Newt, 91
Gohmert, Louie, 129, 164–5, 194–5
Gonzalez, Charlie, 154–5
Gonzalez, Henry B., 53, 154–5
Gramm, Phil, 79
Grand Teton National Park, 87
Graves, Curtis, 66
Great Britain, 51
Great Depression, 48–9
Great Migration, 170

Great Recession, 128
Grover, Hank, 66–7
"GTT" (Gone to Texas migration), 62
Guatemala, 138
Guerrero, Lena, 117
Gulf of Mexico, 16, 51–2, 73, 130
gun culture, 3, 9, 41, 77, 92–4, 123, 169, 200, 213
Guzman, Jesse, 153

Halliburton, 130
Hamilton, Jane, 179
Hammond, Bill, 166
Hance, Kent, 79
Harlan, Doug, 80
Harvard Law School, 19, 24, 154
Havel, Václav, 191
health care, 118, 128–9, 142, 147, 156, 162, 213
Henson, Dr. James, 202
Heritage Foundation, 124
Hickie, Jane, 89, 97
Hightower, Jim, 84–5, 91, 226n8
Hill, John, 75–9, 83–4
Hill + Knowlton Strategies, 88, 225n16
Hispanics, 8, 15, 21, 27, 30–2, 36–7, 52–3, 66, 68, 81, 88–9, 93, 100–2, 118, 133–57, 159–66, 170–1, 174–5, 179, 181, 187–8, 190, 192–3, 197, 219, 222n1
  and the Bushes, 147–50
  demographics of, 137–9
  and Karl Rove, 136–43
  and religion, 145–7
  and Republicanism, 143–7
  and Rosie Castro, 150–7
  and youth, 137
  and voting, 21, 30, 36–7, 81, 159–61
Hobby, Oveta Culp, 51
Honduras, 138
Houston, 8, 21, 36–7, 45, 50–3, 62–9, 75–6, 88, 100–5, 109, 116, 118, 130, 138–40, 148, 150, 165, 170–3, 199
Houston Post, 51, 88
Houston Space Center, 118
Huffines, Don, 122

human suffering, 213–16
Humphrey, Hubert, 67
Hunt, H. L., 44
Hurricane Ike, 16
Hurricane Katrina, 5, 104
Hurricane Sandy, 16
Hutchison, Kay Bailey, 67, 80, 91, 115–20, 125–7, 215
Hutchison, Ray, 75, 116, 118

immigration, 9, 45, 118, 124, 134–6, 160, 163–7, 170, 199–200, 213
income inequality, 5, 213
Independent party, 103
International Brotherhood of Teamsters union, 65
Iowa, 7
Iraq war (2003–2011), 111, 115
Israel, Celia, 150
Ixtoc I spill, 83

J. C. Penney, 61
Jaworski, Joe, 195
Jaworski, Leon, 195
Jewish religion, 162
Jillson, Cal, 114
Jim Crow laws, 46
Johanson, Karin, 25–7
John Birch Society, 44
John F. Kennedy Profile in Courage Award, 104
Johnson, Lyndon B., 3, 49–56, 67, 89, 108, 111, 213, 223n9
Johnson, Phillip, 14
Jones, Alex, 169
Jones, Jerry, 144
Jones, Robert, 161
Jordan, Barbara, 66, 154, 213
"Joy of the Gospel, The" (Pope Francis), 162

Karam's Mexican restaurant, 151
Kazantzakis, Nikos, 216
Kennedy, John F., 43–4, 55–6, 104, 114, 152
Kerry, John, 4, 176–7
Kilby, Jack S., 60–1

Kirk, Ron, 101
Klein, Ezra, 115
KLRU-TV (Austin PBS), 10, 112
Koch brothers, 124–5, 141–2, 170
Krauthammer, Charles, 115
Krier, Cyndi Taylor, 80
Kroll, Andy, 155
Krueger, Robert, 116–17
Ku Klux Klan, 46

La Raza Unida, 150, 153
labor unions, 27, 34, 52, 181
Landry, Tom, 81
Langley, Russell, 177–9
LaPierre, Wayne, 124
Laredo, 101, 139
Latino, *See* Hispanics
Latino Decisions, 134
Lebowitz, Larry, 13
Leininger, James, 124
Lewinsky, Monica, 101
liberals, 10, 20, 23, 38, 44, 51–5, 64,
     66–9, 71, 75, 77–8, 83–6, 88–9,
     94–5, 115, 119, 125, 129, 152,
     159–60, 172, 180, 206, 208, 215,
     221n4
Libre Initiative, 141
Limbaugh, Rush, 121
Lockridge, Joe, 66
Lone Star Project, 37, 178
Lubbock, 79
Luce, Tom, 43–4, 55–7, 59–63, 107–11,
     126–8

MacArthur Foundation, 153
Manhattan Institute for Policy
     Research, 171
Manzano, Dr. Sylvia, 134
Martin, Jack, 78, 84–5, 88, 97, 179
Martinez Fischer, Trey, 150
Mattox, Jim, 84–5, 89, 226n8
Mauro, Garry, 85, 100–1, 139
McClellan, Scott, 103
McDonald, Craig, 125
McGovern, George, 85
McKinnon, Mark, 201
Medicaid, 124–5, 129, 145

Medicare, 124–5
Mexican American Legal Defense and
     Education Fund, 136
Mexican Americans, 45–6, 52–3, 66, 68,
     93, 102, 118, 135–6, 138–40, 144,
     147–55, 166
Michael's restaurant (NYC), 24
Michigan, 6, 62
middle-class, 5, 61, 170–2, 191–5
minimum wage, 68, 124–5, 137, 141,
     213
minority population, 7, 35–6, 39, 64–7,
     139, 151, 153, 171, 173, 179, 196,
     202, 229n1
     See demographics
money, 176–83
"Moses" (Michelangelo), 216
Mostyn, Amber, 16–17, 182
Mostyn, Steve, 16–17, 182
MSNBC, 20
Mullinax & Wells (Dallas), 64
Murdock, Steve, 196
Murray, Richard, 36, 85–6

Nader, Ralph, 76
National Association for the
     Advancement of Colored People
     (NAACP), 52
National Association of State Treasurers
     (Jackson Hole, Wyoming), 87
National Jewish Democratic Council,
     176
National Journal, 172
National Rifle Association (NRA),
     123–4
Nazi party, 130
Nelson, Willie, 205–6
Nevada, 8, 135, 219, 227n27
New Deal, 48–9, 52
New Deal Democrats, 52
New Texas experiment, 90–6
New Texas Way, 159–83
New West, 24
New York, 9, 24, 91
New York, 24
New York Times, 111
New York Times Magazine, 20

Niebuhr, Reinhold, 95
Nineteenth Amendment, 48
Nixon, Richard M., 51, 67
No Child Left Behind, 5–6, 111
"No Pass, No Play," 108
Norquist, Grover, 5, 124
North American Free Trade Agreement (NAFTA), 139
North Carolina, 131, 187
North Texas, 61, 63, 203
North Texas Toll Authority, 61
nursing homes, 155, 192–4, 204–5

O'Donnell, Peter, 56, 63–4, 77, 82, 119
Obama, Barack Hussein, 7–8, 13–17, 20, 25, 34–5, 38, 113–15, 125, 130, 145, 150, 154, 161, 164–5, 181–2, 187, 199–200
"Obama Derangement Syndrome," 115
Obamacare, *See* Affordable Care Act
Ohio, 7, 16, 34–5, 62, 131
oil, 3, 9, 43–7, 50–2, 57, 60, 67–8, 73–5, 79, 81, 83, 85, 90, 94, 101, 112, 117–18, 128, 130–2, 203–4, 221n1
and Ixtoc I spill, 83
and oil boom era, 46–7, 73
"Old Three Hundred," 45

Pangburn, Pat, 14–15, 18, 21, 24–5
Parker, Annise, 172
Parker, Richard, 123
Patrick, Dan, 121, 164–5, 168–9
Paul, Josephine Lopez, 162
Paul, Rand, 2
Paul, Ron, 124
Paxton, Ken, 121, 127, 167, 227n22
Peña, Albert, 152
Pennsylvania, 6, 62
Pennzoil Oil Company, 68, 73–4
Perales, Nina, 136
Perot, Ross, 57, 59–62, 107, 144
Perry, Charles, 129–30
Perry, Rick, 2, 21, 43, 91, 101–5, 111–15, 118–20, 127–30, 132–3, 135, 163–4, 169, 189, 199
and gubernatorial primary (2010), 115–20

"Pete Wilson" moment, 135
Pew Research Center, 146
Pierson, Katrina, 166
"Pit Bull" Democrats, 112
Planned Parenthood, 7, 13, 16, 22, 31
Plano, 61–2
Plouffe, David, 17, 35
Pope Francis, 160–3
Pope John XXIII, 163
populism, 4, 47, 52–3, 82, 84–5, 127
prisons, 9, 125
Proposition 187, 135
Protestantism, 162
Public Broadcasting Service (PBS), 10, 112
public education, 19, 48, 94, 107–11, 144–5, 154, 162, 166, 192, 213
Public Religion Research Institute, 161
Public Strategies, 179

racism, 9, 113–14, 134, 164–5
Randolph, Mrs. Frankie, 53
rape, 19, 90
Ratliff, Bill, 200
Raymond, Richard Peña, 138–40, 143, 190
Ready for Hillary super PAC, 7–8
Reagan, Ronald, 41, 76–7, 81–3, 109, 113, 143–4, 171, 189
Reagan-Bush Texas Victory Committee, 81–2
Reagan Democrats, 41, 189
Reconstruction, 39, 44–5, 50, 52, 66–7, 113
Red Shoes, The, 97
Republican National Committee (GOP), 11, 19, 44, 56, 63, 67, 71, 73, 133, 144, 160–1, 164, 169–70, 172, 176, 181–2, 186, 207
Republican Party of Texas, 41–57, 167–70
birth of modern, 48–51
and business, 43–4
history of, 41–57
and internal conflicts, 167–70
and Reconstruction, 44–8
and the "Texas Way," 44–8

Richards, Ann, 1–3, 10, 15, 19–21, 24, 32, 64, 69–71, 84–5, 87–100, 110, 112, 115–18, 120–1, 128, 132, 134–5, 154, 174, 176–7, 179, 181, 185, 187–90, 197, 200, 202
  and alcoholism, 90, 97
  and frustration, 96–100
  as governor, 87–100, 211–16
  and New Texas experiment, 92–6, 197
  and people as resource, 128
  as state treasurer of Texas, 87
Richards, David, 64–5, 70
right-wing, 9, 20, 23, 43–4, 56, 107–8, 112–15, 119–21, 123–6, 163–4, 167, 169, 172, 206–7, 213–16
  and Christian crusaders, 9, 107–8, 112
  and Republican extremists, 43–4, 112–15, 120–1, 206–7, 213–16
Rio Grande Valley, 36, 68, 100, 102, 139, 141–2, 202
Roe v. Wade, 70, 77
Rogers, John, 11, 70, 75, 152
Rogers, Mary Beth
  and Ann Richards, 1–2, 70–1, 87–100, 152, 211–16
  as CEO of KLRU-TV, 10, 112
  childhood of, 11
  as deputy treasurer, 87
  and feminism, 188–9
  on the future, 211–16
  as "Mrs. Extremo," 152
  and New Texas experiment, 92–6
Rolling Stone, 24
Roosevelt, Franklin D., 48–9
Rove, Karl, 4–5, 42, 43, 81–2, 91, 94, 98–101, 119, 123, 136–43, 201
  and Hispanics, 136–43
  See Texas group
Royal Dutch Shell, 195
Rubio, Marco, 149, 161
"rule of everydayness," 191
Rumsfeld, Donald, 74
Rust Belt, 62, 170
Ryan, Nolan, 81
Ryan, Paul W., 161

same sex marriages, 121–2, 167, 175
San Antonio, 11, 37, 53, 62, 64–6, 68–9, 80, 124, 126, 138–40, 150–5, 162
San Antonio City Council, 53
San Antonio Light, 152
Sanchez Jr., Tony, 101–2, 135, 140
Saveur, 24
Schlumberger, 130
Schriock, Stephanie, 25
Second Vatican Council, 163
Second Wave women's movement, 68–9
SEDCO, 73, 83
September 11, 2001, 174–5
Service Employees International Union (SEIU), 7–8
Sessions, Pete, 174
Sharp, John, 119
Sharpstown Bank (Houston), 68
Shearer, Moira, 97
Shipley, George, 88
"Shivercrats," 51–3
Shivers, Allen, 51–2
Simon, Paul, 139
single moms, 19, 192
60 Minutes, 16
slavery, 45
Smith, Glenn, 88
Smith, Todd, 169
Social Security, 124–5, 145
small business, 41, 61
South Texas, 31, 45, 50–1, 53, 116, 139, 143
Southern Methodist University (SMU), 44, 114
Southwest Airlines, 97
Southwest Industrial Areas Foundation (IAF) Network, 162
Soviet Union, 191
Spindletop, 46
Squire, Bob, 88
Stanford University, 154
Stanley, Marc, 176
Staubach, Roger, 81
Stein, Gertrude, 10
Stevenson, Adlai, 51
Stevenson, Coke, 50

Stewart, Mitch, 7
strategy, 6–7, 11, 17–18, 22–3, 30–1,
    80, 82, 88, 90–2, 97, 119–20,
    132, 149–52, 170, 179, 182, 191,
    197–201, 208, 215
Straus, Joe, 126, 168
Strayhorn, Carole Keeton McClellan
    Rylander, 103
Strictland, Jonathan, 122
suburbia, new, 170–5
Sullivan, Michael Quinn, 123–6, 170
Sun Belt, 62, 109
successful campaigns, 30–2, 41, 99
    and audience, 32
    and flexibility, 30–1
    and the future, 99
    and key warning signals, 31
    and message, 32
    and plan of action, 30
    and strategy, 30–1
    and timing, 30–1
    and white voters, 31
Super Democrat, 189–90, 208
Sutton, G. J., 151
"Swift Boat" campaign, 4
swing states, 6, 8, 16
swing voters, 23, 27, 39, 136, 151, 170,
    190, 198, 201

tactics, 4, 15, 17, 111, 123, 174, 182,
    185, 197–8, 203, 215
TC4 Trust, 141
Tea Party, 3–4, 105, 107, 115, 119,
    121–2, 126, 144, 164–70, 192
Tennessee, 191
testing industry, multi-billion dollar, 6
Texans for Fiscal Responsibility, 125
Texans for Public Justice, 125
Texas, 3, 6, 9, 25, 40–1, 44–57, 107,
    114, 122, 128–9, 213
    complexity of, 3, 6, 9, 25, 40–1
    post-Reconstruction culture of,
        44–57
    economy of, 9
    and educational system, 107, 129
    and government-as-enemy, 41, 213
    and health care statistics, 128–9

and highways, 129
and home-rule tradition, 122
and off-year state elections, 41
and politics as weather, 6
and presidents, 3
and secession, 114
workers in, 128–9
    See Republican Party of Texas; New
    Texas Way; "Texas Way"
Texas A&M University, 173, 177
Texas AFL-CIO, 68, 70, 75
Texas Association of Business, 166
Texas Christian University, 19, 24
Texas Constitution (1876), 45, 65
Texas Democratic Party, 2–3, 82, 105
Texas Democratic Trust, 177–8, 181–2
Texas Democrats, future for, 186–209
    See future for Texas Democrats
Texas Dream Act, 163–7
Texas group (Karl Rove), 4
Texas House Democratic Campaign
    Committee, 181
Texas House of Representatives, 66,
    116, 154
Texas Instruments (Dallas), 60–1
Texas Jew Boys, 102–3
Texas Legislature, 26, 48, 55, 65, 69–70,
    79, 110, 112–13, 121–2, 131, 143,
    150–1, 160, 166–7, 194
Texas Medical Association, 111–12
"Texas Miracle" of job growth, 128
Texas Monthly, 22, 78–9, 156
Texas Observer, 38, 53, 84–5, 125
Texas Office of State-Federal Relations
    in Washington, 97
Texas Organizing Project, 37
Texas Pastor Council Action, 166–7
Texas Politics Project, 202
Texas Public Policy Foundation in
    Austin, 124
Texas Racing Commission, 15
Texas Railroad Commission, 117
Texas Regulars, 49–50, 57, 116
Texas Republican Party, 63, 111, 124,
    168
Texas Select Committee on Public
    Education, 108

Texas State Guard, 169
Texas State Senate, 19, 26, 53, 65–7, 143
Texas Supreme Court, 68, 91
Texas Tribune, 202–3
Texas Values in Action Coalition (TexVAC), 177–81
Texas Victory Committees, 18, 81–2
Texas Victory Fund, 14–18, 33
Texas Women's Center, 69–70
Texas Women's Political Caucus, 70
"Texas Way," 45–8, 52, 68, 76, 79, 93, 102, 188
    See New Texas Way
Tharp, Twyla, 194
Thorburn, Wayne, 82, 118
Toomey, Mike, 111
Torres, Pete, 151
tort reform, 5, 94
Tower, John, 55–6, 71
Treat, Jennifer, 88
Truman, Harry S., 49
Turner, Chris, 26–7, 30, 33, 37
Turner, Lisa, 26, 173–6, 179–81
26th Amendment, 69
Twitter, 19–20
270 Strategies Consulting Group, 7

Udall, Mark, 25, 29
underdog, the, 215
unemployment, 130–2
United Auto Workers, 64–5
United Farm Workers, 68
U.S. Army, 174–5
U.S. Census Bureau, 4, 65, 171, 196
U.S. Constitution, 48–9, 65, 69–70, 122
U.S. Department of Homeland Security, 174–5
U.S. House of Representatives, 3–4, 8, 49, 79, 91, 103, 150, 174
U.S. Senate, 8, 25, 49, 53, 55, 67, 83, 101, 116–20, 185
U.S. Supreme Court, 5, 49, 70, 77, 121–2
University of Houston, 36

University of Texas at Austin, 64, 69, 117, 145, 148, 165, 202
urban areas, 8, 18, 65–6, 122–3, 137, 140, 150, 159, 188

Valdez, Lupe, 174–6
Veasey, Mark, 36
Victorian gentility, 45
Vietnam War, 4
Villalba, Jason, 143–9, 156, 166, 170
Virginia, 7, 187
Viva Kennedy, 152
Vogue, 20
volunteer recruitment, 8, 17, 20, 29, 31, 33–40, 55–6, 63, 70–1, 84, 174, 198
voter registration, 17, 34, 37–40, 63, 231n31

Waco, 64, 204
Weddington, Sarah, 70–1
Wehner, Peter, 126–7
Welch, Dave, 166–7
West, Royce, 180
White, Bill, 8, 21, 38, 40, 104–5, 140, 199
White, Mark, 83, 89, 107, 132
white voters, 21, 31–2, 41, 65–6, 85, 93, 151, 159, 161, 172, 181, 187–8, 190–4, 197, 202, 222n1
Williams, Clayton, 90–2, 94, 99, 110
Wilson, Charlie, 66
Wilson, Pete, 135
wind power, 9
women, 16, 19, 21, 23, 30–2, 36, 48, 68–71, 87–90, 93–4, 96, 98, 116, 118, 129, 164, 172, 189–90, 192, 224n11
World War II, 49, 52–3, 77

Yarborough, Judge Ralph, 52–5, 65, 67, 74, 83–5
"yellow-dog" conservatives, 82

Zapata Petroleum, 73–4
Zorba the Greek (Kazantzakis), 216